Becoming Jesus People Volume 2

More Inspiring True Stories from the 1970s
Jesus People Movement

Carissa Gobble

GPC PUBLISHING

Cover Design By: Nicole Pritchard
Editing: Michael Williams

Contents

Gift For Purchasing This Book

We are so thankful that you chose to purchase a copy of this book and wanted to show our appreciation by making available to you an online treasure - audio recordings of over 550 of Roy's teachings. These can be freely downloaded or simply listened to over the web. To be emailed instructions to access this archive, simply enter your email at the link below or by scanning the QR code.

<u>Roy Hicks Jr Archive</u>

Endorsements

"If you loved the movie, Jesus Revolution, you will find equal hope and inspiration in Becoming Jesus People, Vol. 2. These true stories feature 1970s wanderers and seekers who encounter Jesus for themselves, discovering freedom and love at a radical nontraditional church in Eugene, Oregon. The book also gives a poignant peek into the history of Faith Center's pastor, a man named Roy Hicks, Jr. This is a treat for all those who experienced that era, and a reminder for anyone else that God's work is never done."
- **Eric Wilson,** *New York Times* Bestselling Author of *American Leftovers*

"The testimonies in this book are very powerful, they transported me back to my own time in the 70s running a house that helped support young hippies in their new faith in Christ as was simultaneously happening in Eugene, Oregon as this book shares. Carissa has a talent for telling people's stories. The collection she's compiled in this book will encourage your faith and give insight to that historical move of God I have yet to see the likes of again. Young and mature alike will find an exciting read within this book's pages and come away in awe of how God can transform any life."
- **Alexander Strauch,** Bestselling Author of *Biblical Eldership*

"Carissa Gobble's first book, Becoming Jesus People, created huge momentum into Volume 2. Wow. I was in tears reading the Prologue of Carissa's heartfelt appreciation of where God had planted her to be for such a time as this. You can clearly

see the Lord's footprint in her life all because of her "yes" to do such an undertaking as this one. She has brilliantly captured the stories of a movement in the past that catapulted us into the future we now reside in. The stories within this book will move you, touch you, change you, and bring you insight into where people were and where they are now. Becoming Jesus People, Volume 2, is powerful, and Carissa Gobble was entrusted by God to bring these stories from the unseen to the seen. Well done!"
- **Brae Wyckoff,** Award Winning Author
& President of Kingdom Creativity International

"Employing the same interview approach she and Riley Taylor used in Volume One of Becoming Jesus People, Carissa Gobble has assembled another collection of delightful and powerful firsthand testimonies, this time involving people who were early disciples of Roy Hicks, Jr., pastor of Faith Center in Eugene, Oregon. Deriving from the early years of Faith Center, the testimonies, which include some of Roy's story and the testimony of his wife, Kay, capture well the rich simplicity and core spiritual practices of those days."
- **Steve Overman,** Pastor Emeritus, Faith Center

"While discussing the project of this book with a friend and reminiscing on those amazing days we experienced, she said it really can't be articulated in words and that is true. That is why the style of writing Carissa takes in this book I enjoy because it is not so much about the accuracy of details but is told from what could be interpretation of the thoughts and feelings we went through being caught up in the only true revival in generations, in the U.S. anyways. Hopefully reading this can spark a hunger in our hearts to see God move again in this powerful way."
- **Kay (Hicks) Bourland,** Founding Pastor, Faith Center

"Becoming Jesus People 2 leans into the profound impact Pastor Roy Hicks, Jr. had on a city, a generation, a movement. As one of the seekers who wandered into that funky auditorium in 1973, I am in awe of what the Holy Spirit did in my life and thousands of others. These chapters are a modern memorial to God's purposes fulfilled and a hopeful reminder that He is still working, still moving and still

looking for willing hearts to follow.”
- **Mike Meeks**, Pastor Emeritus, EastLake Church

"Roy Hicks, Jr. was small in stature but large in influence and impact. During his years as lead pastor of Faith Center in Eugene, Oregon, he led the church through an astonishing season of growth that saw thousands meet Jesus and be trained and sent in ministry. Carissa Gobble’s new book tells Roy’s story along with stories of many of those deeply impacted by his life and ministry. It’s a reminder of what God can do when someone dares to surrender, trust and follow."
- **Joe Wittwer**, Founding Pastor, Life Center

“Having experienced the Jesus People movement I’m not sure any of us so-called “Roy’s Boys” knew what being a “Roy’s Boy” actually meant. However, I think all of us knew this: It was among the greatest gifts of a lifetime that we were blessed to be influenced by the life of Pastor Roy Hicks Jr. In Becoming Jesus People Volume 2, Carissa writes in a style that creatively brings Roy’s unique spiritual authority and Holy Spirit sensitivity to life. Roy was the right man, at the right place, at the right time to impact a generation for Jesus. In reading this book, may all of us be Spirit-inspired, and re-inspired by Roy’s example to reach this present generation for Him.” - **Kip Jacob**, Lead Pastor, SouthLake Church

“In Becoming Jesus People Volume 2 God is using Carissa’s style, gifting and anointing to resurrect treasured memories. The life God so sovereignty poured out on our generation was indescribably holy. Carissa taps into the hearts, memories and powerful message of the day. So many began a transformation to Christ likeness from a meaningless existence. That transformation was spread across the Northwest and literally around the world. That anointing continues today with multiple generations. This book will touch your heart and inspire you to embrace God’s intended purpose for your life.” - **Pam Jacob**, Pastor, SouthLake Church

“Thank you for telling the stories. I was of this Jesus people generation. At the time of these events I was already born again and filled with the Holy Spirit. It was my privilege and joy to be close friends and a kingdom coworker with many of those

who were snatched out of the jaws of the enemy who had drowned them in drugs, sex, and cult religions. It is God's way for one generation to tell the testimonies, the stories, the work of God to the next generation. I will paraphrase Ps. 78:5-7. "God creates a story, a testimony in His chosen people, of His praiseworthy deeds, the works of grace and might to establish a testimony. He commands the fathers that they should make known the story of the work of God's goodness and grace to the next generation, so that they would expect the goodness of God's grace to them and their children by not forgetting the things that God has done." Again, Ps. 145:4,7. Vs. 4 NKJV "One generation shall praise Your works to another, and shall declare Your mighty acts." vs. 7a NLT. " Everyone will share the story of your wonderful goodness." These stories in this book do just that. These testimonies cause the reader to be reminded of the mercy, might, faithfulness, love and grace of God that is offered to each generation.Thank you for telling the story and reminding us."

- **Arlan Askew**, Senior Pastor, Westside Vineyard Church

Foreword by Riley Taylor

For me it was a long time dream come true. A year ago this baby-boomer and a millennial co-authored the stories of 19 of my friends and family who ended up living at Liberation House during the amazing days of the Jesus People Movement in Eugene Oregon. In most of the accounts, there was a mention of going to Faith Center and hearing Roy Hicks Jr, because his teaching was so key to our initial growth in the faith. Over the years, I'd always wanted to write about Roy's impact on us. Turns out I had the right idea but the wrong author. The Holy Spirit let me know that this was not my job, that a handoff was called for.

So Carissa Gobble returns with this second volume of Jesus People stories that will encourage your faith and move your heart. She takes a storytelling approach that helps you immerse yourself in the experiences of these believers as they got started and had their first encounters with Jesus. They went on to live lives worthy of the Gospel, walking it out as parents, pastors, missionaries, school teachers, academics, politicians, artists, physicians, lawyers, engineers, counselors, blue collar workers, administrators, business leaders, etc. By 1994 the crowd had multiplied to include thousands of souls in dozens of churches, all established in the faith through Roy or one of the many pastors whom he mentored and released.

Roy's razor-sharp understanding of the Scripture that he taught and the relationship with Jesus which he modeled had the quality of opening for us glistening possibilities of what life could be like living in intimate connection with Jesus. He also walked in an uncanny ability to facilitate the active presence of God as he led worship and post-sermon response times. This man, short in stature, cast a huge shadow in the Spirit. We loved him, trusted him, and were transformed through his influence.

In this second volume I have helped in a small way by connecting Carissa with a new set of people who represent this wider network of saints who encountered Jesus in Eugene. She has performed a true labor of love to interview them and retell their journeys, wherein you get to remember through their eyes. The result is not biography or history, but neither is it intended to be. It is a set of eyewitness accounts passed on to you with the freshness and immediacy of personal testimony.

As I thought about this project, I occasionally had the terrifying image of running into Roy and being confronted with those beady eyes and jutting chin as he rebuked me for making him the hero instead of Jesus. No such intention, Roy! But the fact is that the Father gave us Jesus, and Jesus gave us Roy.[1] I trust you will agree with me that Carissa makes Jesus the star by honoring the gift He gave to us and the Body of Christ.

Long ago Moses stood with the Israelites on the edge of the Promised Land, 40 years after the astounding events of the Exodus. He challenged the Israelites over 20 times not to forget, but "remember"[2] what the Lord their God had done when He rescued and adopted them. Yet most of his audience had not even been alive at the time of those events. So "remember" something they hadn't experienced? What's up with that? The answer is that God was about to lead them into another adventure, ready or not. And He knew they were going to need the revelations embedded in those past experiences. If they would welcome them, meditate on them, they would own them. Well, God is still up to something, and if we're up

---

1. This seems to be the thrust of Ephesians 4:7-16

2. See the book of Deuteronomy.

for it, He's pointing us forward. Jesus is still the light that shines in the darkness. And always overcomes it.[3]

So I encourage you, as you marvel at, get choked up by or laugh at these recountings, let them help you to "remember." My fellow elder saints of my generation, please hear this out of Hebrews: *Remember* your leaders, who spoke the word of God to you. Consider the outcome of their way of life and *imitate their faith*.[4]

And to Carissa's generation and every generation, I exhort you to *remember* what the apostle says next: Jesus Christ is the same yesterday, today and forever.[5] What He did in these tales is the low water mark of what He is ready to do today, in us and through us.

---

3. John 1:5

4. Hebrews 13:7

5. Hebrews 13:8

Prologue

November 19, 2023 - Faith Center – Eugene, Oregon

Tears streamed down my face and I wiped them away, trying not to draw too much attention to myself. The entire worship this morning I'd been crying. Little bits at first but now I couldn't stop it. If it wasn't for the two strangers to my left and the Purkeys and Riley to my right in our pew I'd probably have made my way out of the sanctuary for a minute to collect myself. There was a weighty presence of God doing something in me and I didn't quite know how to process it. It wasn't the music, it wasn't the people, it was the knowledge of how this church had gotten here. It was knowing the legacy behind the space I was standing in. And knowing its story had been entrusted to me to tell.

I watched the teens and children worshiping with their families during the special "One Family" service we'd happened to join today on my research trip to Eugene. Did they know the story? Did they know they were enjoying the fruit of a historical movement of God? It was hard not to envision the people I'd interviewed in these same pews forty years ago. When Roy Hicks Jr still taught from that very stage in front of me. I could see his exit door he'd designed at the back of the stage, and wondered at the "in the round" fish bowl design of this auditorium. Had it been inspired by the "sanctuasium" next door? Were the stair step pews at steep inclines a nod to the risers they'd had on the gym floor in the seventies?

This space wouldn't exist without real people's stories. Without their many "yes" commitments to Jesus, and that's what got me the most.

The tears came again and I didn't care. The magnitude and weight of the privilege I'd been given. To be the one to bring these stories to the world. That Jesus would entrust me with them. That these people would let me steward the narrative of their origin stories in the faith astounded me. How had I gotten here? Probably through some small yes's of my own. And also some no's. Had I ignored the Holy Spirit's nudge to decline that Netflix production job in 2020, I would now have a share of an Oscar on my resume. But these stories would still be dormant, perhaps shared verbally but not preserved in print.

Why God chose me, someone who didn't even exist when these tales were unfolding, still amazes me. Maybe it was because He had helped me to see the gold in them and to honor them like He did. To recognize they still held truth and encouragement for the next generation and beyond. That I could bring them back like memorial stones. With my small skill set, I could celebrate what God did, starting with a small church of fifty people, and with a small man who walked in large authority.

Much like the first book this volume contains testimonies. Mostly from the 1970s time period. The connecting thread now is the church Faith Center and its pastor, Roy Hicks Jr.

As I stood in the new auditorium of this church it was hard not to picture myself transported in time back fifty years as an invisible silent observer to the life and love that abounded and to feel somehow supernaturally connected to it. Because without this place and discipleship houses like the Liberation House depicted in the first book, I'd never have heard my godparents' stories and been enraptured by them. I'd never have asked them to bring me to Eugene and show me the places they were talking about. I'd never have suggested to Riley in September of 2022 that we write a book together. And I never would've imagined the new friendships and connections I've gained through that book's publication.

Each story in this second volume is near and dear to my heart because each story is a person's testimony and showcases how intimately the Lord knows exactly who we each are and how to woo us to Himself. May these stories inspire you as much as they did me. And may they be not just a trip down memory lane but also an encouragement to take up the baton and finish the race these people started. How amazing is it that we still have these mothers and fathers in the faith with us today to share their wisdom and experience with us. Their triumphs and their failures. How many of these stories do we all share in common as the human condition and find Jesus Christ as the answer to it all as we all continue to grow in our own process of .....*Becoming Jesus People.*

rolled up and stopped, a door opened on its side and a chef inside asked if I needed a ride.

"Ya can you take me to Santa Cruz?" I hopped in the front seat.

"Sure can."

I should pray. I looked at my hands. This was the end, wasn't it? If I put those two hands together my whole being would disintegrate into thin air! Don't pray. Bad idea. Just look at the road. It will pass. The drugs will pass.

"Here you go it's just a mile up this road but I gotta keep going man." My driver dropped me off not far from where I'd spent the night last night with those Jesus Freaks. My bare feet hit the hot asphalt and I watched them melt into a puddle. This wasn't happening! Just keep walking Stefan! Just keep walking! I zig-zagged my way up to the house a mile further on, and knocked on the door, panting for breath.

"It's you again. You don't look so good." The guy I'd met yesterday opened the door.

"I need help." The room was spinning. My body was still melting away, staining their carpet with skin and bone.

"Do you want us to pray for you?"

"Yes! Whatever it takes!"

He laid his hand on my shoulder and closed his eyes. "Jesus, come deliver this man of his affliction. Heal his mind and his heart."

The room stood still. My breath and heart slowed. My body was whole!

I stared at my feet. They weren't melted! What had just happened! I wasn't high anymore. I looked up at the man who had prayed for me. He was smiling.

"Welcome back."

The Next Day

I sat on the cement floor of my brother's garage running my hand over my recent buzz haircut. The Bible the Christian commune people gave me yesterday lay open in my lap somewhere in the New Testament. The words leapt off the page at me. Jesus was real. My patriotic veteran brother could hardly believe his eyes when my long haired hippie self had showed up at his door this morning looking for a place to stay. I hadn't wanted to do the whole commitment thing at the commune, so I'd had to leave. My brother's conditions were less strict. I had to cut my hair and change my clothes. So I'd done it. I didn't have any other place to go.

I couldn't deny something had happened yesterday. Some power of God had rescued me from the worst trip of my life. One instant I'd been high to heaven come and the next I'd been sober. It was near impossible, yet here I sat, reading words that didn't make much sense but felt alive somehow. It was saying something in here about believing in the Son of God and not perishing. I recalled some of my minimal Catholic exposure as a child, and the various tracts that kept appearing everywhere I went these past few months. The Son of God was Jesus. He was the way to eternal life. I set the book on the floor, closed my eyes and put my hands together in prayer like I'd seen the priests do.

"Jesus, I believe in You. I don't know what else You need from me but I want what's in this book. I want You. I believe God raised You from the dead. You can have my life."

A dog barked in the neighbor's yard and a strange restful peace crept over me like a warm bath soothing aching muscles that had been tight my whole life. Sinking deeper and deeper into my innermost being.

I opened my eyes.

God had heard me!

1972 - Eugene, Oregon (One Year Later)

"Do you want to go to "Phaze Center" with me Stefan?" my friend Robin asked after I shared with her my salvation story and my desire to return to Eastern Europe. I wanted to go to Poland and Russia and hand out Bibles in the Red Square. I didn't care if I didn't come back this time. Jesus was worth it. He'd changed my life. That book was changing my life! A phase center sounded groovy. I'd be up for that! Maybe we'd get to witness to some people that were just as lost as I had been. I didn't care about the rejection. Any soul saved was worth it all! I had been just one hurting soul searching for a cause in all the wrong places.

"Sure. Sounds great!"

We hopped in her car and drove to what looked like some sort of school near a Seventh Day Adventist church. We made our way down a narrow sloped hall with windows into what may once have been a gym. Two basketball hoops still hung from either end. It was set up like a church! Faith Center, not Phaze Center!

There was a simple melody song played on the piano and then a young man probably not much older than myself got up and opened the Bible to teach. I had never heard such insightful teachings in the Catholic Church I was brought up in. I hung on every word. I pulled out my own Bible from my bag and read the referenced passages as if seeing them in a whole new light. I'd loved this book but so much of it was foreign to me. I didn't understand these principles! The service ended and Robin introduced me to her spectacled friend.

"Stefan, meet Dan Purkey."

"Hi." I took his hand in greeting.

"Robin said you're looking at going into missions?"

"Ya but I don't think I could teach anyone about the Bible the way that guy just did. Those scriptures had always confused me and yet the way he explained it was so simple! It was like how had I not seen that?!"

Robin smiled at my hungry enthusiasm.

"If you want to stay longer you can come over to Liberation House for a few days. We have room."

"Really?! I would love to stay. I need this in my life right now!"

"Great! Robin knows where it is. She can drop you off when you're ready." Dan gave a little goodbye wave.

"You're going to love Lib House, Stefan." Robin and I headed back to her car.

A Year Later - Colorado Rocky Mountains

The familiar presence of the Holy Spirit filled the car in the momentary silence between arguments with this girl driving to Chicago with us. Her name was Bonnie. She was catching a ride home with us over the school break but she'd pushed back on every faith filled thing we'd said, touting the women's rights issues and everything. The sun was setting and the clouds were alight in a blaze of God's glory. Dan had been driving for hours and we were getting close to where they would drop me off for the missions conference I was going to. After a year of discipleship at Lib House, getting baptized by Don Smith, and sitting under the teachings of Roy Hicks Junior, I was ready to pick back up my heart's desire to reach the nations with the good news of the person of Jesus.

Glen, my seatmate to my left, piped up. "Dan, I think I have a tongue." He must be feeling the same presence in the car.

"Ok let's hear it."

Glen burst forth in words I didn't understand but there was power with them.

"Is there an interpretation for that?" Dan asked.

I sensed a line of thought in my own mind and spoke it out loud. "All that you look upon I have created. I have made it for you to use in coming to Me.... Come to Me my child. My love for you is great." The inspiration left and I stopped my interpretation.

I caught a tear streaming down the girl's eye in the rearview mirror. Something had shifted. Maybe she had felt the Holy Spirit in the car too. I hoped she would find the freedom I had. Lib House had its rules but it had taught me self control, and given me a real love of people and the Lord. There were constant scriptures being memorized and we lived out what we were learning. Telling everyone we could. There had been a demonstration recently against the ROTC building on the U of O campus and I knew the frustration and anger in the protestors eyes. I had once been them, but now I was different. Now there was this thing so deep in me I couldn't deny it. A boldness for truth and love that had shifted from its rebellious ways to one of loving others and introducing them to a savior.

This was a whole new cause to fight for but not one we used as weapons of war with, but rather weapons of the spirit. I prayed softly under my breath that this girl Bonnie would come to know this herself, too. It was life transforming and I hoped God would use this trip to capture her heart as He had mine.

Now GO. I will help you speak and I
will teach you what to say.
Exodus 4:12

For I will give you words and wisdom
which none of your adversaries will be
able to resist.
Luke 21:15

Stefan went on to serve with the Slavic Gospel Association in 1974 and we went to France where he took a VW bus load of Bibles and clothes to Romania, Hungary, and Yugoslavia for three months. To this day he continues to fight in prayer in the spirit for the advancement of the kingdom of God in this next generation. He still carries the boldness of the spirit and shares his faith with others, praying for clients, healing when they share illnesses with him. Stefan married in San Mateo, California in 1975. He and his wife Patti now live in Redwood City, California and attend The Bridge Foursquare Church. They have two sons.

You can read what happened to Bonnie in the first book. You can read Dan's and Glen's stories in the first book as well.[1]

Lib House outing climbing South Sister. Pat McCormick on the left Stefan on the right.

---

1. Carissa Gobble and Riley Taylor, "Becoming Jesus People:True Stories of How Love Broke Through In The Jesus People Movement," (GPC Publishing, 2023), 33-78, 9-12, 45-52.

In front of Lib House. Stefan in middle standing holding a Bible.

Chapter 2

Roy's Story Part 1

1958 - Omaha, Nebraska

My hands connected with the bottom of the slimy garbage can as the bullies dumped me in head first. "Try to get out of this one, Shorty!" they yelled as they dispensed my five foot two inch frame into the receptacle. Someone slammed the top down, not even connecting with my shoes as I tried to kick back. "THAT'S NOT MY NAME!" I yelled at the top of my lungs but then felt something wet and papery connect with my nostrils. Yelling upside down was a bad idea. The stench of expired lunch meat hit me like a brick. This was a no win scenario. Breathing through my nose or mouth, it didn't matter. Something unsanitary was bound to get in my airways!

I tried kicking but to no avail.

"God! Why did you make me so short?! Please, please, please just give me six more inches. I beg you!"

I started rocking myself back and forth.

If only I could tip this thing over I could crawl out.

I guess this is why that kid had come up and embraced me wearing the freshman beanie on my first day of school and said, "I'm so glad I'm not the shortest one here any more!"

We hadn't become friends in the past few weeks. I'd just become the newest target of the upperclassmen and their wretched initiations. I was going to give them a piece of my mind!

The can wobbled...One more push!

I slammed as much weight as I could towards the teetering corner and felt the whole thing tip.

Clang!

Crash!

"Ow!"

My elbow and shoulder had taken the brunt of the fall. I was on the ground, the blood rushing back from my head with the pull of gravity. "Bless them which persecute you; bless, and curse not.....Recompense to no man evil for evil."[1] My dad's authoritative pastor's voice rang in my ears alongside the vibrations of the crashed can on the asphalt. Avoiding as much decomposing gunk as I could, I started scooting myself out the now open end of the can. Mom would not be too happy about my clothes when I got home. She had her hands full these days with my toddler sister Lorrie. My younger brother Jim would probably laugh. He didn't have to deal with this kind of thing.

The light of day greeted me and I blinked back tears of pain.

It wasn't fair!

---

1. Romans 12:14, 17a

Standing up, I braved a glance down at the gross prison I'd been thrust into a moment ago.

Maybe this was a bit like Joseph felt in the Bible.

Being thrown into a pit.

A rotten banana peel was stuck on my pants.

No, I think this is worse. Ancient pits didn't have rotting bananas in them.

I picked off the peel and other trash I found attached to my person.

This wasn't something I'd anticipated dealing with now that we were settled in a home and not traveling by trailer, preaching in different cities up and down the east coast anymore. I thought it would be nice to be settled in one spot vs wandering nomad style as we had for many years. Dad had gotten special permission to homeschool us as we'd traveled.

I uprighted the trash can and put the lid back on it, resisting the temptation to just leave it there so someone would know there had been mischief afoot. Visual validation of the emotional and physical pain I'd just endured.

Those jerks. Bullies!

The adrenaline was slowly leaving my system. I spotted my cornet and book bag in the grass a few feet up the alleyway. Those bullies had better not have broken my instrument! I picked it up and inspected it. It didn't seem to be damaged. If there was any bright side to this, like there was in Joseph's story, I couldn't fathom it. What good could God do with me being so short. I hated being a pastor's kid. What good can come of getting "canned." The cornet in my hand brought back memories of those traveling trailer years with my family again. Those really had been the greatest times. Touring all the old civil war sites with my brother Jim. Putting our fingers in the bullet holes. Making praise music with my mom and brother and dad on all our own separate instruments. Could I go back to those days? Growing up was overrated.

I slammed my book bag over my shoulder. Unscathed cornet in hand, I started the trek back home. A friend on a bike sped past me and waved. We'd gotten in trouble a few times together. I ignored him, completely absorbed with my anger. Could I get back at them somehow? Was it possible? Reporting them to the principal would probably just make more trouble. Roger was coming in a few days. Dad had asked him out here, probably concerned about me.

"Bless them which persecute you…" my dad's voice echoed in my brain again.

Really not feeling it…

I closed my eyes and paused. The anger was slowly abating. I didn't want it to. I wanted to hold on to it and wrap myself in it like a cozy blanket. I was infuriated! I wasn't that same kid from a few years ago that had given all my newspaper route earnings to the visiting missionary, unprompted. I'd forgone a bike I'd been saving for for months because I'd been so moved by their mission. Nope, I wasn't that kid anymore.

1964 - Angelus Temple - Los Angeles, California (Six Years Later)

Shame crept its fingers around my gut as the last moments of the day's sun lit up the towering stained glass windows of Angelus Temple. I'd chosen the farthest place up here in the third balcony next to a big pillar. No one would expect me to walk down three stories for an altar call. I'd participated in more altar calls than I could count, starting with one at a revival meeting Mom and Dad were attending outside our home in Ohio when I was nine, and a powerful baptism in the Holy Spirit at age thirteen.

I knew Jesus. I'd even started the Bible college thing as expected after high school but dropped out last year and moved down here to L.A.. Ed was a good friend and this city and job at the District Attorney's office was growing on me.

Some of the people in the rows of red upholstered seats in front of me headed out to the stairs weeping. Touched by the Spirit, or conviction, no doubt. Headed down to the altar. Well good for them. My gaze drifted to the large rafters that held up the domed roof. This wasn't my first time here. Many years ago my buddy Tom and I had pranked the pianist Chelsea by climbing up the beams and yelling down to her that she should go to China. She couldn't see us and was visibly shaken. We'd gotten such a great laugh out of it but she hadn't been so thrilled when she found out. Those were the days...

I understood now why the Bible said "And be not drunk with wine, wherein is excess; but be filled with the Spirit."[2] Some of these people really did look like the friends I was meeting at parties down here with Ed. I got the appeal of it now. This life was different than I was used to as a pastor's kid. Inside I wrestled with two paths. Go back to LIFE Bible college? Or start studying law.

The people around me were growing sparse. I felt exposed.

But I am liking this change of pace in life, God! I really am drawn to the life of a lawyer. I don't want to be down there on a stage like the one two stories below me where Aimee Semple McPherson, the founder of the Foursquare Movement, once stood. I don't remember it but I'd been told Aimee herself had dedicated me to the Lord. What an ironic full circle decision moment I found myself in. Pastoring and Bible college. It's just... I don't think I want to go that route.

The preacher below shared another emotionally appealing call to repentance and more of my seat neighbors stood up and headed out. Conviction seeped its way into my heart. I was being laid bare. Here I was, all the way up here, drawn by the familiarity of church and having heard so much about the origins of the Foursquare movement growing up, that I had wanted to come back to Angelus Temple across from Echo Park Lake with its swaying palm trees. So different from the topography and climate of Canada where I had been living previously.

I really was practically alone up here now. If I stayed much longer the preacher would surely call me out. I stood up and made my way to the large pillar support-

---

2. Ephesians 5:18

ing the dome roof of the theater-like sanctuary. Yet I felt like I should stay. Process my choices. Law or Church? Using my God given gift with words to promote justice or follow in my father's footsteps towards a life of ministry?

My eyes closed as I let these realities sink in.

I had to choose.

This space, this atmosphere, felt so much like home to my spirit. It contrasted with the life I'd started living down here. Church felt right and intimidating all at once.

Someone walked down the steps behind me and stopped.

"The Lord is telling you...do not turn to the right or the left,"[3] a male voice spoke.

The hair on the back of my neck stood up and all the shame and conviction that I'd been stuffing down and trying to avoid with my rabbit trails of thoughts hit me full on. I spun around to see who had just confronted me and a middle aged spectacled man smiled then shuffled down one of the rows of seats to my right. I couldn't hold back tears any more as I left my hiding place and sat back down in my seat.

My head in my hands I surrendered. I knew better.

I knew better than to join in on the parties and the drinking. I knew, deep down I knew the answers to my own questions. I knew God was calling me to the ministry. A strong, clear direction settled on me. Yes. I needed to return to Bible college. "God forgive me..."

That warm comforting presence I hadn't felt in a while started to swallow me whole until all the questions faded. All the irritations and frustrations from school faded. The religiosity I butted heads with frequently. The know-it-all professors. The academia that made Jesus a topic on paper versus a living person

---

3. Proverbs 4:27

active in my life. What about all the hurting people I saw in the D.A.'s office? Who would reach them? Or the beautiful people in South America I'd met on short term mission trips growing up?

You can reach the whole world Roy, through the local church...
That still small voice.

I knew that voice.

"Ok God." I looked back up at the altar full of hurting people finding a savior. Finding Jesus. There was representation from all ethnicities down there. Jesus wasn't a respecter of persons. Maybe I didn't have to do things in some of the religious capacities Bible school seemed to promote? Maybe there could be a turn to this. To relationship. Helping people find a real relationship with Jesus. Could the church be more than a building and religious liturgical exercise? I'd seen it outside the four walls of tradition growing up on the road with Mom and Dad. Could people be led to the person of Jesus instead of denominations? I knew my faith was real. I knew Jesus was real. What if there was a different way to be a pastor?

I turned around to find the man who had bravely delivered that prophetic word of the Lord a moment ago. Our eyes met and he nodded a knowing smile on his face. I smiled back.

God had drawn me here, not ready to let me go. The least I could do was surrender and say yes.

Summer 1968 - Camp Crestview - Corbett, OR (Four Years Later)

I couldn't take my eyes off of Kay's enrapturing face. She was beautiful and had the sweetest smile I'd ever seen. Yet she looked at me with a serious cold shoulder stare. My heart sank, and the cool Pacific Northwest forest breeze blew into the lunch hall we were sitting at. Had I mis-interpreted what I felt the Lord was telling me the moment our good family friend Norma Mourer had mentioned the beautiful English teacher that had gotten saved at their church last year?

When summer camps had started I'd been ecstatic to find out Kay was here for the summer serving as a camp counselor. After that one date we'd been on a few months ago I'd known it. This was the woman I was going to marry! Yet she'd rejected my offer of another date and seemed to avoid me for the first week or so here at camp. Those had been the hardest nights...

I'd given God an ultimatum as my heart felt like it was breaking. "God if she won't have me, I'm going to be single for the rest of my life!" I couldn't imagine my future anymore without this woman. She wasn't the first girl I'd been on a date with. There'd been quite a few girls I'd dated since returning to Bible college and then taking the Youth Director of the Northwest District job with the Foursquare Church. But I'd known on that first date, maybe even before it, that Kay was the one. But now she showed no interest. She almost seemed intimidated by me sometimes.

God what am I going to do?! There she was sitting at the lunch table with the rest of the leadership team giving me the coldest look yet.

I stood up.

I needed to try again.

I was so sure.

I kept eye contact and she didn't look away as I moved down the table to face her. "Kay, we are headed over to play some ping pong on break. Will you play a match with me?"

Her eyes widened then softened. "Why not."

Did she really just say yes?! My love-stricken heart skipped a beat.

"Great, I'll see you in a few!" I said a little too enthusiastically. She just nodded and took a bite of her lunch as I turned away and made a beeline for the game hall before she could change her mind. Hope flooded back into me and I couldn't help the smile that crept over my face. I'd made headway! Now I just had to get my competitive gaming spirit under control to milk this opportunity for as much time as it could give me with her.

October 1969 - Shiloh Discipleship House - Eugene, Oregon (One Year Later)

My nose had grown accustomed to the body odor. This was like no Bible study I'd ever seen. And I'd seen a lot. My dad had even done church in a drive-in theater when I was a kid. Unconventional church wasn't a new thing for me but there was life here. I sat next to my new bride Kay in the seats at the back they'd pulled from the kitchen for us. John Higgins, the house leader who'd come up after living with Lonnie Frisbee in Southern California, was having people share their testimonies. I scanned the room where we were all packed in like sardines in this Christian communal living home that had been seeing what could only be described as a movement of God. I'd been hearing about this from some of the other local pastors in Eugene. I'd wanted to see it for myself.

We'd only been here a few months. Roy Mourer, the Foursquare District Supervisor, had offered my newly married self the chance at pastoring a church. As much as I'd embraced my calling to the ministry, the Youth Director role in the Foursquare church wasn't really for me anymore. The traveling to Montana and Wyoming and Washington states had gotten tiring now that I was married. I'd told my dad and Mourer, "I'd just like to serve a church of fifty people that will love God and love each other." I wanted to help grow big people, not big regions. Bring people into encounters with the person of Jesus.

We'd been hoping to pastor a church out in Bend but then came to visit the small one here in Eugene and I knew it was right.

This little church had been through some stuff before we'd gotten there. Its numbers had dwindled but I loved the small intimacy of it. It was small in structure too, and we lived on the property, with a curtain separating the living area from the Sunday school rooms. One of the Sunday School rooms had been transformed into our own bedroom. The first time I'd walked through the place alone I'd taken down the weekly attendance and giving report board. This wasn't going to be a numbers church. Even the name didn't mean much to anybody so I'd approached the council with a name and logo change suggestion. They graciously agreed.

A new wave of body odor hit my nostrils, bringing me back to my surroundings as a young man took the empty seat next to me. Crusted food was housed in his foot long beard. They were called hippies. Considered the underbelly of society, a rebellious youth with no morals. Stuck in a cycle of drugs, political advocacy, and free love. Yet here they were talking about Jesus. The woman sharing right now about a genuine encounter she'd had with the Lord was clearly not wearing a bra but the tears on her face were real. The presence of Jesus here was tangible. There was something happening here.

My thoughts drifted from the woman's testimony to Pauline, the pianist at our new church. She'd come up to us a few weeks ago and told us that she'd had a dream there was going to be a revival in Eugene, Oregon so she'd moved all the way out here a few years ago from the midwest. I wonder if this is what her dream had been about? A picture of the "CHURCH ON SUNDAYS - COME AS YOU ARE" sign Dad had hung under the drive-in movie theater marquee we used as a church when I was a kid came to mind.

Come as you are.

I turned to the guy sitting next to me, "Hey are you going anywhere for church on Sundays?" I asked as the meeting ended. He looked down on me from his six foot height. "Nah, me and my girl tried it once. They tried to get me to wear deodorant and I wouldn't have it. This right here is church enough for me." He gave me a grin.

"Well why don't you and your girl come to the church I pastor this Sunday?" Kay stood up next to me and smiled up at the young man as well. He gave her a little nod. "You pastor a church?" he asked, his eyebrows raised. I knew I wasn't much to look at compared to some preachers. "Yes, it's called Faith Center."

He combed his beard contemplatively with his fingers then held out his hand for a hand shake, "Alright man, we'll come try it." I shook his outstretched hand.

<u>Roy's story continues in Chapter 11</u>

1957 Roy holding little sister Lorrie with brother Jim.

1966 Roy's Trio, Roy on the left.

Chapter 3

I Don't Want to be a Pastor's Wife

Kay's Story

1966 - Portland Foursquare Church

"**I**f you don't know where you are going when you die and you want to, I invite you to come down and receive Jesus." Pastor Mourer ended his sermon and I eyed my boyfriend to my right. He wasn't moving. Probably because he knew he was going to heaven when he died. Of course he would. His parents had raised him in church. But what about my parents...

Mom and Dad weren't together anymore. Mom was with her boss now. A new couple. It had not been a pretty break. Was divorce ever a good thing? Would they go to heaven or hell? What would happen to them if they died, having gone through this disaster of morality. The minute I'd been confirmed at their episcopalian church in California we'd stopped attending, even when we'd moved to Kailua, Hawaii we'd never visited church. I'd even gotten my teaching degree from Pacific University in Forest Grove, Oregon and never really heard anything like this before. But I did know right from wrong. I wasn't one of the counter cultural people, I was a good girl, the hippie life held no appeal but I did like this guy sitting next to me. He'd brought me to church three times and now I was so full of fear for my parents' souls.

I found myself standing up and making my way down the aisle to respond to the altar call. The pastor met me by the podium. "Do you want to know Jesus?" he asked with a kind smile on his face.

"No, I'm just concerned for my parents. I don't know where they will go when they die. There has been some infidelity in their marriage. What will happen to them?" I asked.

He motioned me to sit down on the steps of the stage beside him so we could talk further and I obliged. My heart was drowning in concern.

"What's your name?" he asked.

"Kay. I'm a teacher." I offered.

"Well Kay, we can definitely pray for your parents but what about you? Do you know where you are going when you die?" He redirected the question.

I wasn't here for me, was I? "Well... I'm not sure, pastor."

"Would you like to be?"

I didn't actually know. I loved teaching other people things but how had I gotten all the way through college and not known this important piece of information. Where would I go when I died? Something in me knew this pastor spoke the truth. There was a heaven and a hell. But what could I do about it? "Yes I think I do want to know."

"Well it's real simple. You confess your sins to Jesus, confess with your mouth that He is the son of God, believe the Father raised Him from the dead, and ask Him into your heart to stay. Would you like to do that with me?" He opened his hands as if in invitation to something so simple my school students could do it.

Was that really all it took?

No big performances or rituals?

"Ok."

Should I kneel? I should do something. Isn't that what they did in churches with a pastor? I transitioned from sitting on the steps to a kneeling posture as the pastor continued. "Then just repeat after me, Kay."

I closed my eyes and didn't miss a word. Repeating his prayer verbatim. My soul was on the line here. Finishing with "Jesus come into my heart and stay. Amen." I felt a lightness descend on me.

Is this God?

The sounds of other congregation members singing or talking faded.

Everything went black.

"Kay! Are you ok?" Voices awakened me.

My eyes fluttered open and I found the pastor, with a concerned look on his face.

What had just happened?

I pushed myself up to standing amongst the others kneeling at the altar in prayer.

"I think you passed out. Your head fell on my knee at the end of the prayer," Pastor Mourer filled me in. "How do you feel?" Genuine concern was in his voice.

I felt fine.

More than fine.

"Different. I don't think I have words to explain it." I lifted my arms up, turning them over and then brought my hand to my forehead. I didn't have a fever. I looked normal. But something was completely different. I looked back at the pastor and people around me. My boyfriend was nowhere to be seen. The pastor smiled. "Welcome to the family of God dear sister Kay."

1967 - Banks Highschool - Banks, Oregon (One Year Later)

Knock, Knock, Knock!

Someone was urgently hammering my closed and empty school room door. I looked up from my desk to see Betty Powell smiling and waving at me through the thin door window. I got up to let her in.

What was she doing here after school? She didn't even live way out here. It was at least a forty-five minute drive from Portland. And her son that had taken me to church with him a year ago where I'd gotten saved, well we weren't together anymore. I was dating a coworker now, a handsome teacher here at Banks high school.

"Hi Mrs. Powell. To what do I owe the pleasure?" I gave her a short hug and welcomed her in.

"Kay it's good to see you." She took a seat opposite my teacher's desk and I started moving some papers aside to create a more hospitable space between us. "Have you read that story in the Bible about David and Bathsheba?"

My hands froze mid movement of the papers.

What kind of visit was this?! I looked up and met Betty's gaze.

Did she know?

Better just go with it. "Yes I did read that one. Wasn't it in the old testament? Kind of reminded me of what my mom did." I put the papers down and rested my hands in my lap.

"It was such a joy Kay when you got saved last year. We were thrilled. I know you had a genuine encounter with Jesus."

Where was she going with this? I knew this too. I'd been the one to experience the radical shift in my life after that night and seen how her son really wasn't living the

Christian life. We'd ended our relationship and I'd also gotten filled with the spirit not too long after my salvation night. Some kind of new boldness had gripped me a little while later and I'd found myself sharing the gospel to a friend for thirty straight minutes! I didn't know where that had come from. Had to be the Jesus in my heart. I still felt so new to this faith and it had kind of slid a bit these past few months. A bad feeling started to seize my gut. I didn't respond and Betty continued.

"But now I hear you're dating a married man Kay. Your friend's husband to be exact! Do you know what happened to David? Do you remember the story in the Bible? The severe consequences God wrought upon Israel and their wayward king because of his immoral choices?"

My whole body was frozen now, that bad feeling washing me in shame and fear.

What was I doing? My new found faith, although genuine, hadn't fully transformed my life.

She must've seen the impact her correction was having on me because her firm tone changed to one of sympathy.

"I know this is what happened with your mom, Kay. But it doesn't have to be what happens to you. This isn't who you are. You know better than this now. You are a new creation. I just couldn't stand by and watch a dear new sister in the Lord get waylaid by the plans of Satan." She reached across the massive oak desk and grabbed my cold clammy hand.

What's that term the Bible used so often? Fear of God? Is that what this was?

So much of that book felt foreign as I'd jumped into it this past year. Thees, thous, and other old English words even I, as an English teacher, had had to look up a few times to understand. But there was life in it. I knew it was truth. Just as I knew right now she was here scaring me with promises of real doom if I kept up this improper relationship any longer.

"I know you'll make the right choice dear." Betty's voice brought me back to the present moment.

I couldn't speak so I just gave her a scared little nod as she got up and left the room.

How did I get here?

I mean, I know how I'd gotten here. A friendship. A smile. A hug lasting longer than necessary. There was another tap at the door and I looked up to see the man in question in the doorway. His attractive features that had drawn me in now seemed so scaly.

Before I could think I heard myself say out loud, "I'm done. I can't do this anymore."

He looked confused, oblivious to the conversation I'd had moments ago that had convicted me to the core. I got up and shut the door in his face.

"Jesus forgive me."

Sitting back down at my desk I felt a relief wash over me like water on a hot day.

1968 - Camp Crestview - Corbett, Oregon (One Year Later)

Pong. Smack! Pong. Smack!

I put my full weight into the swing of the paddle and sent the white ball clear into Roy's section of the table, scoring another point! Claps erupted around us in the game hall. I knew Roy was competitive. How was I winning right now? He was probably letting me win.

He picked up his paddle and sent the ball back my way with a knowing smile.

That same smile he'd given me at Hillsboro Foursquare Church months ago when he'd asked me out on a date. He'd heard about my unique conversion experience from the Mourers, and when he'd come to speak at my church I'd returned to, after Betty had confronted me a few months prior, he'd asked me out.

It had been a really awkward date. He challenged me about who my healer was when we discovered we'd both been in recent car accidents and still dealing with residual pain. Also he was a little intimidating. Bold even! He shared the gospel with our waitress and I felt so unequally yoked to this young man who'd been raised a pastor's kid and was clearly on a track for church leadership. I wasn't cut out to be any kind of pastor's wife. I couldn't play the piano! I barely had a few verses under my belt. For all intents and purposes I was a baby Christian and he could be my grandfather in the faith for how long he'd known Jesus. I'd even barely gotten back on track because of Mrs. Powell's convicting visit.

Ping! The ball went over my shoulder and Roy got a point. I needed to bring my thoughts back to the present and not embarrass myself here. I picked up the ball and sent it with determined force back across the table. Here at camp the counselors like myself didn't get many breaks to play games like this between batches of students visiting. I hadn't known Roy would be here when I accepted the summer role. This job worked well since I was off from teaching but as soon as he'd seen me he'd asked me out again. Of course I had said no. Yet he was persistently trying to hang out with me and get to know me and what he saw in me other than my attractive femininity I didn't know. There were at least five other girls here intent on winning his affections. Why didn't he pay them any attention? They'd make better pastor's wives. I didn't want to be all about a husband's ministry like I'd heard wives talk about. "My husband is called, not me," they'd told me at church multiple times. And they played the piano. I couldn't do that. I didn't want to do that. I wanted God to use me, not just as a husband's support.

So no. I'd said no.

"Kay, you're up three points!" one of the other female counselors came up beside me and brought my focus back to the game at hand. Roy was still smiling at me. A strange warm and caring sort of feeling sneaked its way into my heart. To be so sought after by him was sweet. But the logic in my brain told me it wouldn't work. I didn't want to resent a husband that was in ministry all day. I wanted to know I was called to something like that too. Not just following a husband's calling.

He sent the ball back and we had a nice solid back and forth run for another three minutes before I scored again and the game ended. I'd won.

"Good game, Kay." He came up and shook my hand.

"Ya, maybe we should do it again next week," I suggested, as a sort of peace offering.

His kind demeanor changed at my words to a look of pure glee at the prospect.

"Absolutely!"

I put the paddle down on the table for the next person to play with and walked out of the game hall to get alone with my thoughts. Why had I just encouraged him? Why had I done that? Was he wearing down my walls? I had asked God for a sign a few nights ago.

I walked back to my cabin and sat on the bed and closed my eyes. A warm presence settled on my heart I'd come to know was the presence of the Holy Spirit. Just last night I'd felt it when I'd prayed for one of my friends who was ill and she'd gotten healed immediately! That same warm presence had filled the room then that was here right now.

I used you Kay...Just you, last night. I called you. I will use you.

The revelation hit me like a warm summer wind. He had worked a miracle of His sovereign grace through my little faith last night. That wasn't anything to do with a husband. It wasn't anything to do with a pastor's calling. That was just me and Jesus. The sign I had prayed for.

I opened my eyes as the warmth faded as softly as it had crept over me. Roy's face filled my mind's eye. Maybe my fears were naught. Maybe my inadequacies were irrelevant if God was with me. If God was in this relationship opportunity.

My cold hard walls seemed to melt before the truth that I had a personal testimony of God using me without any superior Christian husband at the helm. Maybe I shouldn't write Roy off.

I closed my eyes again and inhaled deeply.

"Ok, God. I won't say no. I'll stay open to this, no matter how I felt initially."

1969 - Faith Center - Eugene, Oregon (One Year Later)

Roy walked me back past the stage after service to our little living space in the chapel building we pastored, staring at me with those beady brown eyes that made my knees weak. My feelings had caught up with our whirlwind relationship this past year. Strange how I could say yes to God and the emotions and passion came afterwards. Our little dog Jericho greeted us enthusiastically. I was thankful he hadn't run out onto the stage during Roy's sermon this morning. The congregation didn't mind but it was a bit interruptive.

Our living area attached to the Sunday School rooms was a cozy little place for a newlywed couple to start out. My laundry still hung on the bedroom doors drying from yesterday's wash since I didn't have a dryer. We'd almost gone to Bend but then our visit to this little church had felt right. The people were pretty gracious with the changes Roy was making. Some had left but for those that left a dozen more showed up. We were starting to feel the cramped quarters, and the unpredictable visits from parishioners needing help or a place to stay were making the space feel smaller. Amazingly I never felt neglected as a wife. You'd think as things were growing exponentially and people needed more of Roy that I could get left out, but he was always there. The same at the pulpit as he was in private.

We worked well together. I was growing so much in my own faith being in his family. Of course it wasn't perfect. A few minutes into our marriage we'd had our first fight and my insecurities had come up. I'd told him he married the wrong person, he should've married his previous fiancé, Joyce. We'd prayed through it and bound the enemy and he'd come back to me the next day and told me God had convicted him saying, if he succeeded in changing me he would no longer love the one he married. So he left any changing in God's hands.

He'd been true to his word. He really had let me find my way. He'd suggested I teach Sunday school, knowing I wasn't going to play piano like a normal pastor's wife nor did he expect it of me. And Sunday school was a perfect fit. I loved teaching! I didn't know much of the Bible at all yet so most days I just recycled what I heard Roy teach and catered it to a younger age. He was so patient with me. Even when I made mistakes. He just had to look at me with that look he'd get if I really had messed something up and conviction would roll right in and I'd know I needed to fix my mess. Thank God I'd said yes to this man.

This thing happening in our church right now was starting to feel like a roller coaster ride. Yet somehow there was grace. *I am still in control Kay, even if it feels like there is no order to your life right now I'm here.* The Rhema word of God speaking to my spirit in only the way He could came back to me. I'd been staring at similar laundry when I'd heard it like a silent comforting voice in my head a few days ago. It had filled me with a faith that could only come from Jesus. He was with us. There was a gift of faith for it even in all the things that were happening we hadn't expected. Somehow despite the many wandering lost souls that were finding their way into our little cramped chapel, we were thriving. We weren't overwhelmed. We were right where we were supposed to be and I couldn't wait to see what else was in store.

December 1977 - Roy & Kay's Home - Eugene Oregon (Eight Years Later)

I walked into the house and saw Helen Baker holding my newborn son Jeff in her arms and the insecurity washed over me again. How had I become a mother? How could I be a mother! I didn't have a good example in my own mother. I was an only child. I'd never taken care of an infant yet here was my one month old son in one of my dearest friend's arms and she was a natural. Like us the Bakers hadn't been able to have kids. They'd lost a baby before term and I couldn't imagine the pain.

I took off my coat to distract myself from the motherhood task before me. The Bible study I'd just led had been wonderful. There were plenty of wonderful mothers there. I didn't think I could be like them. Just these first few weeks had been an education! Diapers, bottles, lack of sleep. Physically it was a lot; emotionally more so.

Just six weeks ago I had put away the paperwork to apply at the adoption agency for kids in Asia. It wasn't going to work out. Days later in church a sudden desire to be a mother had washed over me like I'd never experienced in my life. It was so strong I had blurted it out to the dear lady sitting next to me like some sort of revelation.

"I want to be a mother." I whispered it again, now trying to remind myself of the miracle this baby was. Within two weeks of me surrendering the adopting from Asia idea and my motherhood instinct surfacing in church, we'd gotten the call. There was a baby born on Halloween in the hallway of a Kaiser hospital in Portland. Did we want him?

Roy and I had intuitively known this was our baby. We drove up there after Roy had ended his sermon holding up little booties, announcing to the congregation in the gym that we were going to go get our son. Jeff had slept the whole drive down and we were in total awe of the miracle God had done to give him to us.

The memory brought a smile to my face as I walked over to Helen to take Jeff from her arms. Ron and Helen were God sent friends and now godparents to our baby. Helen shifted his bundled sleeping frame into my still nervous arms. The wave of insecurity still stuck in the pit of my stomach.

You will share him like you do your husband.

I sat down on the couch and held back tears.

It was that Rhema word of God again. Meeting me in my vulnerable moments with a fresh comforting word to my soul. He was right. This child wasn't mine alone, just like Roy wasn't mine alone. This baby had a calling on his life. He was the Lord's. We just got the privilege and call to raise him. I didn't have to be the perfect mother because I wasn't mothering alone. God was with us in this just as He was with us in leading the church which had grown beyond our wildest dreams. That word of faith that had anchored me that day staring at the laundry on the door in the old church came back to me now. Jesus knew me so well. He knew exactly what to tell me to combat the lies of the enemy. He knew I could handle the call on our lives for ministry in this thing that could only be called a movement. He knew my background and life before I knew Jesus didn't matter when it came to the things he was setting before me now to do and be. To be a mother was a gift, and I didn't have to walk it in isolation or draw on my own understanding to do it well. Jesus would be with me like he had been in so many other ways.

> *Finally, brethren, whatever things are true, whatever things are noble, whatever things are just, whatever things are pure, whatever things are lovely, whatever things are of good report, if there is any virtue and if there is anything praiseworthy—*

meditate on these things.
Philippians 4:8 NKJV

Kay and Roy's church continued to grow in leaps and bounds. You can read more about it in chapters 11 and 21, as well as upcoming chapters. They adopted their son Jeff in 1977. A few years later Roy stepped down as lead pastor at Faith Center and was working in L.A. While Roy was commuting home to Kay and Jeff, Kay underwent a mental breakdown from the stress of travel, speaking engagements, and lack of sleep. Roy returned from work in California to be with her as she regained her health. You can read about Roy's processing of this experience in his book "A Small Book about God."[1] Kay instantly and miraculously recovered.

You can read Ron Baker's story in the following chapter.

Kay in her twenties.

---

1. Roy Hicks Jr, "A Small Book About God," (Colorado Springs: Multnomah Books,1997).

Kay and Roy on a trip to Israel.

Roy and Kay on the left. McConnells on the right for an
Anniversary.

Chapter 4

Saved From the Draft

Ron's Story

June 1964 - Army Recruitment Office - Portland, Oregon

I sat on the cold faux leather vinyl patient bed in the army doctor's office awaiting my glucose test results that would determine the course of the rest of my life. Would I be eligible and physically fit for the draft and sent to Vietnam? Or would this second glucose test also come back indicating I could have diabetes. I'd come a few weeks ago after graduating high school and not passed the test so they'd made me come back. What a way to start off the rest of my life. Either getting drafted into a war while our country was in chaos, president Kennedy had just been assassinated last year, or I was facing a diabetic health crisis. Which was it going to be?

The door opened and the doctor walked into the room inspecting a clipboard I supposed had my blood test results on it. I froze. This was it.

"Well son, looks like we are still getting the exact same results as we did the last time you visited. You'll want to follow up with your family doctor back home and get help with these diabetic signs. You need to take this seriously. As far as we are concerned though you'll be designated 4F, so you're free to go." He put his clipboard down, smiled at me, then walked on to the next young chap awaiting his fate.

I relaxed a little. The worst of the options had been eliminated. But now I had to figure out what was going on with me. I pulled on my jacket, careful to glide the sleeve over the bandaid the nurse had applied after drawing my blood. A small price to pay for getting a 4F status. That meant they wouldn't be calling me unless there was some dire emergency in our country that would warrant someone with a medical handicap jumping in to defend it. Not likely going to happen unless Russia actually nuked us.

I was lucky I guess? But diabetes didn't sound so great.

January 1967 - First Christian Church - Eugene, Oregon (Three Years Later)

The lukewarm water was up to my waist as Reverend Dr. Carlton Buck stood next to me in the baptismal. My girlfriend Helen with her raven black hair and stunning brown eyes that pierced my soul was beaming as she watched from the pews. I was here because of her. We'd been dating a few years now and she'd brought me an ultimatum. Get baptized or hit the highway. I had accepted Jesus in my heart at twelve years old sincerely. My mom had made me come to church every week with my twin brothers growing up but for some reason I'd never taken this step. Helen's zeal for Jesus and strong faith was part of what attracted me to her. Of course I'd get baptized.

"Ron, because of your confession in Jesus I baptize you in the name of the Father, the Son, and the Holy Ghost." Reverend Buck said and I lost the next few words as he submerged me in the water. I closed my eyes as my head went under and then it was done. He pulled me back up to a standing position, water dripping everywhere. The congregation clapping and letting out a few "Bless the Lord!"'s was sweet to hear. I blinked the water off my eyes and climbed out of the tub.

They were all so happy for me. Joy filled my heart as I accepted the towel Helen handed me with the biggest grin I'd ever seen on her face. She was delighted.

Inside I felt equally delighted. Or was it something else. No. It was something else. It felt special but there was this clean feeling I didn't recognize occupying a space in my heart I hadn't known needed cleansing. I wasn't super in tune with how my body felt if the false diabetes diagnosis was anything to go off of. I'd followed up with a civilian doctor after my visits to the draft office and they couldn't find anything wrong with me. Said it must've been a fluke.

Wrapping the towel around me, realization dawned on me.

I'd been saved.

Jesus had saved me. Not just my soul but also my body.

Somehow I had not passed two glucose tests with the army but I had with my own doctor and been spared the trauma of the draft and war. No diabetes in sight!

Tears welled in my eyes as Helen hugged me with my wet clothes, towel and all.

This new internal purity was shaping my view on my world and circumstances.

I owed Jesus my life.

1974 - Eugene, Oregon (Seven Years Later)

"Ron!" My wife of seven years, Helen, yelled my name as her nurse Sherri Ar-buckle helped her hobble back into our home, back brace still intact, after a Bible study she'd taken her to. Helen had been in an accident and required significant surgery a few months ago. She still had a few months of the neck and back brace that required her to either stand or lay down. My wife was such a solid believer in Jesus her faith in trials like this inspired me. I wouldn't have wanted to go to a new Bible study if I was in such a state. But Jesus was everything to Helen. Sherri had been the sweetest nurse during Helen's hospital stay and had invited her to a Bible study by this lady Brenda Berg from a church in town called Faith Center.

"Ron, we have to go check out Faith Center. You won't believe this but there were one hundred women crammed into Brenda's house for this Bible study! They were the kindest creatures! Sherri asked them to help me find a place to lie down so I didn't have to stand the whole time and the whole crowd parted for me and cared for me the entire time! The conversations were so significant and insightful! I'm going back next week for sure and we need to check out their church!" Even in her neck brace Helen's outgoing personality couldn't be held back.

"Ok, sure." I agreed. If a Bible study could get Helen this excited even in her invalid state I was super curious about this church.

A Few Months Later - West 24th Ave

Helen's bike came to a screeching halt and I almost catapulted into hers on mine.

"Ron, it's Roy & Kay's house!"

I un-straddled the bike to balance myself and followed her gaze to the small home to our right with curtains in the windows, and a Rolls Royce parked in the driveway. It did look like Pastor Roy's car I'd seen them get into after services at Faith Center where we now attended. It had taken one visit to this church after that Bible study Helen had gone to and we were enraptured by the teaching and multitude of people our age in the place. We were loving it.

Before I could respond Helen pushed her bike up to the porch of this little home.

"Come on, let's go say hi!"

"What?!" I didn't want to bother the pastor and his wife. What was Helen thinking! She was bolder than me, it was true, but why did we need to push ourselves into their lives right now? There were probably plenty of other people who truly needed their attention. But Helen was already knocking on the door, not waiting for my answer as I stood still, frozen in the street.

Maybe they won't be home? I hoped.

No such luck. The door opened and Kay Hicks the pastor's wife appeared with her long blonde hair, sweet smile, and floor length dress. She hugged Helen and invited her in. Roy appeared in the doorway and waved to me. I had to respond now.

I raised my hand a little and waved back, unsure what to do. Helen smiled at me in her knowing manner and then disappeared inside the house. Roy was putting his shoes on. Was he coming out!?

I panicked. What could I say to him? Was he really coming over here to see me? Did he even know who I was?

I un-straddled my bike and pushed it onto the sidewalk so I would appear to be less of a gawking cyclist in the middle of the road as my new pastor approached. He was about my age, but what would I say when he got here? What do you talk to pastors about?

"Hey it's Ron right?" He offered his hand.

"Ya, Ron Baker." I took his hand in greeting after leaning my bike against the nearest tree.

"Did you see the Duck game last night?"

Wait, was this guy really asking me about my favorite team?

"Ya, ya, it was really something." Maybe I would find something to talk about with Roy after all. "Have you ever been to a track and field meet on campus?" I asked.

"Not in a while but I'd love to go sometime. Is there one coming up?"

"Yes! I'm volunteering when the Olympic trials come rolling into town for them in a few weeks."

"No way! Could I come watch?"

"Absolutely. I can get you the details on Sunday."

"That sounds amazing Ron. I love sports. I also love my wife's sandwiches. Would you like to come in and have lunch with us?"

He'd totally dismantled my fears in a one minute conversation about some of my most favorite things.

"Sure."

"Great! Why don't you come park your bike over here by the porch next to your wife's and we can head inside."

I obliged, wondering how we'd just ended up in a casual lunch with our new pastors, unplanned.

Helen is why. My amazing, wonderfully brave, wife.

"Ron, do you guys play cards? Like Hearts or Spades?" Roy asked as we walked up the steps and he opened the door to their little home.

"Yes we love card games, although it's kind of hard to play with just the two of us."

"I know. Kay and I have the same problem. Do you have time this afternoon? Maybe we could try a game or two with the four of us after lunch. Although we'd probably have to partner with each other's spouses so whoever loses doesn't get an earful from us later." He chuckled as we joined the women in the kitchen.

Maybe we had more in common than I originally thought. I had been so amazed in this guy's church how he would teach from the word things that made sense and were practical and applicable to my growing relationship with Jesus. His services weren't like the normal ones you'd see in a pentecostal style church either. He valued order and didn't let someone just waylay the flow of our time with a random word in tongues in the middle of his sermon. But then he also had discernment on when to get interpretation for it. Or when to just worship and then let the congregation go home early because that's all he felt the Lord had for that day. It blew my mind that this short pastor around my age would also be so down to earth and have so many similar interests that I did. Maybe there was a friendship waiting for us here I didn't expect.

1975 - End of Service - Faith Center (One Year Later)

My best friend was giving the altar call that ended the service and I got up to check with Maynard Coleman about our disruptive friend from earlier in the evening we'd had to usher out. It was a Sunday evening service and people were already filtering out the double doors at the back of the gym. At least a dozen or two people had responded to Roy's invitation to meet Jesus tonight. It was typical of a service these days and I loved the gifting in my friend to follow the Lord's leading.

"Hey, Maynard, what happened with that guy?" I asked our bulky friend who was the dedicated bouncer for visitors that would get disruptive.

"It was awesome Ron. Tim Morgan and I prayed for him after bringing him outside and were able to minister to him and he left healed! It was amazing." Maynard was grinning. Not all our disruptive visitors had such great endings. Sometimes we had to threaten to call the cops. As an usher it was part of my responsibilities to help in these scenarios but Maynard took the hard cases. A lot of times it was the drugs talking. Other times you might even be doing deliverance in the parking lot over someone. I don't think we ever did end up having to call the police but it got close sometimes. Not everyone liked what God was doing here. Or their friends had gotten saved and they came mad wanting to get back at us. I was glad tonight's incident wasn't a really hard case.

I'd ushered at our previous church but this job entailed a lot more than that one with how many people and services we navigated now. The church kept growing. I spotted Stephanie Skeie as she exited the sanctuasium with a Bible clutched to her chest. I waved and she came over.

"Ron, you are friends with the farmer that Lib House picks chickens for right?"

"Yes we are."

"Oh my goodness Ron, you won't believe it, the whole crew went over again four nights ago and I was still picking feathers out of my hair before church this morning! That job is nasty!"

"They so appreciate you guys coming and doing it Stephanie. They really do. You guys are such troopers to take on that job as a house."

"I know it's for a good cause. It is a great character building tool for the new folks in the house too. But still, I knew you knew the owners so I had to come share that with you. Goodness it's awful work but it's unto the Lord and we sing through it always!" She smiled and gave another wave as she joined up with her friends.

Helen came up then, with Kay and Roy not too far behind. "Let's go get some Taco Bell and head over to the Hicks for a game of cribbage," my wife suggested. Roy came up then and gave me a brotherly side hug.

"How did that situation go earlier Ron?" He asked.

"Maynard took care of it. Said the guy left but not before they had a chance to minister to him and he even got healed!"

"Praise God," the three of them all said in unison.

"Well that sounds like it's worth celebrating with a Taco Bell dinner." Roy smiled.

"Let's just not get any slushies this time," Kay joked as she looped her arm in Roy's.

I laughed. She was referring to our trip up to Portland a week earlier when we'd stopped in Salem and gotten Icees at the gas station. Roy had a need for speed in his life and unfortunately I had put the drinks in their container on the dashboard in front of me. Well those drinks had ended up all over my lap after his first acceleration, as we got back on I-5. I shivered at the memory of the ice cold liquid drenching my pants for the last 40 minutes of our trip.

"I think I owe you a new pair of pants, Ron." Roy smiled.

"It's fine, really. It all washed out fine."

"I did have to run it through two cycles of the wash though, dear." Helen corrected me as we four walked back to our cars.

Roy stopped us before we got much further and turned to Helen. "You don't feel good today do you?"

I looked at my wife's countenance. How did he know? I could tell a little bit, but how on earth could Roy tell? We didn't talk about our stuff with them. They were our best friends and when I needed spiritual support with something I didn't want to infringe on those times with them. I'd go talk with Stan Brown when I had a spiritual or life question. Helen was amazing at masking her feelings. No one knew when she was having a bad day. How did Roy know?

Helen nodded silently under Roy's caring gaze.

"Let's pray." He put his hand on Helen's shoulder and said the simplest prayer request of Jesus to be her strength. I guess he could tell there was something troubling her spirit. It was amazing to me. I'd never had friends like this before. Real friends. That knew us so well. Roy was fast becoming the best friend I'd ever had.

"Thank you," Helen said as the prayer ended and we made our way to our respective cars.

As I started the engine Helen pulled out a new book from her purse.

"Another recommendation from Roy?" I asked.

"Yep. He said it was a good one. Handed it to me at the beginning of the service while you were helping everyone find seats."

I smiled. The last book he'd given us he'd said the same thing. And he was right, it was a good one.

How sweet was this life we lived now. I could never have imagined it.

For God so loved the world that He
gave His only begotten Son, that who-
ever believes in Him should not perish
but have everlasting life.
John 3:16 NKJV

In the coming years Roy & Ron's friendship grew. Ron has been described by others as Roy's best friend. The two couples would fly together for dinner to Sunriver. Kay & Roy made Helen and Ron their son Jeff's godparents. Ron worked as head usher for many years at Faith Center. He volunteers at the track and field olympic tryouts at the University of Oregon every four years except for 2020. He still participates in cribbage club on Thursday nights in Eugene. He and Helen still attend Eugene Faith Center and have been married for 56 years. They continue to be part of Kay and Jeff's lives significantly.

1980 Helen & Ron

Ron, Roger, and Roy 1989

Chapter 5

Carrot Juice & Prayer

Mary's Story

Summer 1968 - Officers Club - Ashaffenburg, Germany

"Danke," I thanked the waiter as he handed me the boot full of beer straight from the tap. All my brother's co-workers in their army uniforms stared at me with mischievous smiles as I held the communal cup. It didn't matter I was only fifteen. In Europe the smallest kids drank beer. Here goes nothing.

I tilted the massive boot up by the toe and found myself washed in the bitter suds that only halfway made it into my mouth. They all burst out laughing and my brother handed me some napkins.

"You have to hold it by the heel when you take a swig, Mary." He took the boot from me and demonstrated. No spills. I on the other hand was a total wet brew mess. At least beer here tasted better than the stuff I'd been introduced to back home in the States. My parents had sent me here because I'd been too much trouble. The past year had been terrible at home. I think they hoped time overseas would be good for me. So here I was after living with my oldest brother Craig for a month, who was in the Air Force now. I was staying with my other brother, Ken, who was in the army. But here I was, still exposed to alcohol. Not sure my parents had thought that one through.

I tried my best to dab up the cold brown liquid as the officers all went back to their jabbering about work stuff or what they were going to do when they got back home. I wasn't sure what I'd be doing either, except heading back to school. I'd blown up my world with a simple poem last year. It was a school assignment I titled "God if you did this, then why did you do that." I'd needed one more line so I put "why did you make my dad see another woman while my mom sat home to wait." I'd gotten an A on it and proudly brought it home, passing it around to my parents and their visiting friends to read. I didn't understand their silence and lack of congratulations until the next day. The foster girl that lived with us pulled me aside and asked why I hadn't shared what I knew about my dad with her. "We tell each other everything!" She proceeded to tell me that my mom's best friend, Maureen, had come over before I got home from school, proclaiming that my dad had an affair with another woman, and wondered how I had found out about it. I was stunned. It wasn't true. It was just a poem. But word spread fast and people started asking questions about how I knew. And soon I discovered what I'd written in that poem was actually true. The pain of the foster girl rubbing it in had been too much. My brothers were away in the service and I couldn't talk about it with anybody.

"You ready to try again?" Ken asked.

The boot had made its way back to me.

"Ya." I wasn't going to stay the laughing stock of the evening. I replaced my hard shell over my inner distractions and took another drink.

"Huzzah!" They all cheered as I drank without making a mess this time. The bitter brew was warming me from the inside out and displacing the troubling thoughts from home.

The men returned to their conversations except for one sitting to my right, Dave. He was smiling at me in that knowing way. "Mary, you want to dance with me?" he asked discreetly, while my brother was distracted talking with his neighbor.

"Sure." I took his hand and we headed to the dance floor. I was flattered that a grown man had asked me to dance. The cool wind from the open doors to the patio was refreshing after the internal warmth the beer had caused.

"How much longer are you in Ashaffenburg?" He asked.

"Just a few more weeks."

"That's a shame. It would have been nice to see more of you." His eyes were captivating. Wasn't this every girl's dream? To get twirled around in a foreign land by a soldier in uniform? No parents in sight? He led us out to the patio in step to the live music. For all the trouble I'd caused at home I couldn't have imagined a more magical visit to Europe. Dave pulled me in closer and slowed to a stop.

"You have the most enchanting eyes Mary." He stared at me with passion and I froze. His hand inched up my arm and then cupped my chin. Before I could breathe or move, his lips were on mine. It wasn't my first kiss. I'd been kissed last year at the school dance by another boy named Dave. What was with Dave's and kisses? But this one was way more passionate, his other arm circled my waist pulling me in closer.

"DAVE!" My brother yanked me away from his friend's embrace. "What are you thinking!" He stared at his friend in disbelief. "She's fifteen!"

"What?!" Dave's shocked expression was almost comical. "She's almost as tall as me! How is she only fifteen?! Dude you better keep a better eye on your little sister!" I was really tall for my age at five foot nine inches. We were also all pretty much drunk. It was an obvious mistake.

"YOU better keep your hands to yourself!" My brother yelled over his shoulder. "Grab your coat Mary, we are heading home."

I obeyed but inwardly I couldn't wait to tell my girlfriends when I got back to the States! I'd just been french kissed by a soldier in the army! I doubt any of them could claim the same...

1970 - Oregon College of Education - Monmouth, Oregon (Two Years Later)

"Mary?" the resident assistant Becky called through the door. Shoot. I snuffed out the joint, and tripped over the blanket on the floor on my way to the door. I grabbed the air freshener and sprayed it five times before removing the tape around the door frame we used to keep the hall from knowing about the dope in our room. I opened the door.

"Yes, Becky?" I attempted a smile.

"It's popcorn night! Come down to my room." She gave a wave and walked back down the hall. I should go. Becky was kind enough she never reported us even though I knew she could tell what we were up to in here. I didn't want to give her a reason to change her mind. I shut my door and joined the other girls in her room.

Two bowls of popcorn were getting passed around. I snagged a seat near Louise, a girl I'd known in high school and had recently turned on to the gloriousness that was pot. I took a handful of popcorn and passed the bowl to the next person.

"I want to read you guys something," Becky pulled out a Bible and I froze with puffed kernels filling my mouth. I knew she was a Christian but I didn't want anything to do with religion. She started reading. "Look unto me, and be ye saved, all the ends of the earth: for I am God, and there is none else."[1] Stick with it a bit Mary. Don't be rude.

---

1. Isaiah 45:22

My dad had taken us to church for awhile when we were really little, until the church had offended him by going with a different realtor than my dad on a building purchase. He had put so much into the research for them, only to be dismissed. We hadn't gone to church after that. My dad was amazing. He loved us so well. I still reeled over the revelation of his affair I'd gotten at fourteen.

Becky continued to read as I finished my popcorn. Flashbacks to the fear I had when the foster girl that lived with us had taken me to visit a pentecostal church when I was ten years old came back to me. There were people rolling around on the floor screaming and marching around the building like the story of Jericho in the Bible. They thought I'd been filled with the spirit and that's why I was crying but I had really just been terrified. I shivered at the memory. It still haunted me. If that was what faith was all about, I didn't want anything to do with it.

I stood up, determined. "I'm not going to listen to this garbage any longer. Let's get out of here." I made eye contact with half the room I knew would follow me and then stomped out the door. I heard at least five pairs of footsteps behind me. Good. They'd be better off looking for meaning, like I was, in things like Hinduism, Buddhism, or astral projection than that old book.

A Few Months Later - Darcy's Health Food Store - Eugene Oregon

I shoved the stubborn carrot into the juicer with determination. This machine was not going to get the best of me! I could at least juice carrots if I couldn't figure out what I wanted to do in this life. I'd dropped out of college and been working for Darcy in her health food store the past few months. How I'd happened to get a job with a hard core Christian boss I didn't know. Seemed like I couldn't escape this stuff. I'd even caved one night in Becky's room and prayed a prayer with her although I didn't know if I really meant it. It had kept her off my back.

The carrot gave way and the machine whirred to life, spitting out orange liquid from the other end. I did love the carrot juice we made. It was pretty amazing. I just didn't think I wanted to be here forever. Was this my lot in life? Making juice? What was I going to do?

Darcy kept telling me all these wonderful things about her faith that didn't seem to match up with my other experiences of Christianity. What if there really was something for me in it. She was a wonderful woman. She'd made a business for herself here. She was always giving credit to God. Was it possible, after I'd looked into all the other religions, that this one I so opposed might actually be the answer?

The ridicule my boyfriend had given me when I'd told him I'd prayed with Becky a few months ago still stung. I couldn't try the Christian God if he was still in my life. But I liked this boyfriend a lot. Would it be worth it? I couldn't keep up like this much longer. I had to have direction in my life and this was one I hadn't tried yet.

I put the carrots down.

A sense of decision washed over me. I fell to my knees as my hard outer shell cracked a little and the soft inside made itself known. "Ok Lord, if I'm supposed to receive you, break up me and my boyfriend." I hoped that counted as a prayer. I couldn't explore this road with my boyfriend criticizing me, we were a great couple with no issues at all. If we broke up, I would know God was listening..

October 1971 (One Year Later)

"We are over." I threw the napkin on the table and stomped out of the restaurant. It was my birthday and we'd gone out to eat and I'd had enough. Things had become rocky in our relationship the past few weeks and I was finished.

"But Mary!" I heard his voice fade as I exited the restaurant and rushed home. It had happened; that thing I'd asked God to do. I ran into my parents house that I'd moved back into after quitting school and up the stairs to my room before they could see my tears. I fell on my face on the floor. And the waterworks burst.

"Ok Jesus. You can have my heart! You can have my heart."

There was a pool of tears on the floor. I wiped away the tears on my face and searched for that Bible Becky had given me a long time ago. I found it stashed in a dark corner of my closet. It opened to Psalms 8.

> When I consider Your heavens, the work of Your fingers, The moon and the stars, which You have set in place; What is man that You think of him, And a son of man that You are concerned about him? Yet You have made him a little lower than God, And You crown him with glory and majesty![2]

The tears came back again and I reread the passage over and over hoping to sear it in my brain. He had made the universe yet still he was mindful of me! Still he chose to crown me with honor! What was this?!

The Next Night

I headed out the door with my Bible in my arms.

"Where are you going?" My parents asked.

"I'm going to Bible study."

Their jaws dropped and I didn't wait to hear their response as I walked out. They probably thought I was lying again. They knew it was a habit I'd had for ages but I was telling the truth this time. In fact I was going to always tell the truth from now on. It's what God would want me to do. I made my way a few blocks to where Becky lived and knocked on her door. I knew it was their Bible study night and I needed more information.

"Oh, hi Mary!" Her smile didn't waiver no matter how many times I'd brushed her off when she'd shared this stuff with me before.

---

2. Psalms 8:3-5, NASB

"Becky, I have received the Lord now. And I want you to tell me everything you know about Jesus."

She looked like she might cry and I didn't want to start more waterworks of my own after depleting the reservoirs last night! "Can I come in?"

"Yes! Please do. I'm happy to share!" She opened the door wide and I entered.

1972 - Liberation House - Girls House 19th St. (One Year Later)

I pulled out the chicken feathers from my socks. How I'd gotten chicken feathers in my socks last night chicken picking with the Liberation House crew while wearing boots, I didn't know. It was the worst experience. It took days to recover from the gunk that filled our eyes and nostrils as we loaded chickens from the farm into a truck every couple of months. It helped pay for the discipleship house operating costs that Louise and I were living in. Well sort of living in. We had the upstairs apartment since we were both students at the University of Oregon. Louise had gotten saved not too long after I had. Most of the girls in the house weren't students. As much as I hated chicken picking I couldn't help but appreciate how well it served as a character building tool. All of us working together doing some gross disgusting and difficult things while simultaneously singing songs of praise we'd been learning at this church called Faith Center.

I picked out the last feather and tossed it in the trash. I needed to find Laurie, the house shepherdess. I made my way downstairs.

"Laurie?"

"I'm in the kitchen!"

I found her drying the dishes.

"What's up Mary?"

"I was just wondering about the new people that keep coming to the guys and girls houses. I feel like we can do a better job in welcoming them when they first come in. Is there any way we can make it more hospitable? I mean like I think everyone just thinks someone else is going to talk to the new guy or girl."

"Hmmm...." Laurie finished her last dish and turned to me. She knew I loved sharing my new faith. I'd told everyone I knew about it since that tearful birthday night. It seemed like everyone I knew was coming to know Jesus! It was incredible. This discipleship house was great. The church we were going to was so welcoming to all different kinds of people. I was getting to know Kay and Roy Hicks, the pastors. Their church was small when I'd first gone there but now we'd just moved into a remodeled school to accommodate the massive growth.

"How about this." Laurie's voice brought me back. "The next new person that walks through the door, *you* get to know them." She smiled at me.

I could do that. Maybe my observation of lack of engagement with the newcomers was the Lord trying to prompt me to be the answer to the need?

"Ok, I'll do it!"

The Next Week

The new guy sat there on the bench. I was going to do it. It was dinner time and we all ate together at the men's house. Laurie's words rang in the back of my head and also Roy's sermon from Sunday about loving one another as God loved us. I was learning so much in that church! I was brave! I could do this.

I plopped my plate next to the new guy. "Hi, my name is Mary."

I must have startled him. He didn't respond right away.

"Hi." He put his fork down on his plate. "I'm Russell, but you can call me Russ." He held out his hand and I took it.

"Well Russ, it's great to meet you. Welcome to Lib House!"

"Thanks." He picked up his fork again.

"What's your testimony? How did you meet Jesus?" I asked.

"Well I wasn't really looking for him."

"This sounds interesting already!" I wasn't nervous anymore. How could one be nervous meeting people that were all going through the same thing. Encountering Jesus. Changing their lives around. Leaving the draw of the world for the draw of Heaven. Abandoning the love of the world and all its counterfeits for the love of a Heavenly father that would pursue us through our lives and even our rejections. "Please continue Russ." I took a bite of my dinner and was all ears.

> *"But if we hope for what we do not see,*
> *through perseverance we wait eagerly*
> *for it."*
> **Romans 8:25 NASB**

Mary and Russ married ten months later. They served on staff at Faith Center for a few years and then planted a church in Monmouth, OR with their two year old son. Their son became an instant magnet for new mom relationships and Mary had so many opportunities to share Jesus with other women. In 2008 they moved to Florida to plant a church there. Three years later they moved to Boulder and pastored the Boulder Foursquare church for eleven years. Now they reside in Denver where they continue to participate in a house church ministry. They have two kids, four grandkids, and one great grandchild.

You can find Louise's and Laurie's stories in Becoming Jesus People Volume 1.[3]

You can find Russ's story in the following chapter.

Lib House van, Mary is smiling second from the right.

*Mary & Russel McCall "chicken picking" during their time
at Lib House.*

Chapter 6

Orchids & Architecture

Russ's Story

1968 - University of Florida Campus - Gainesville, Florida

I heard the clock tower strike one-o-clock and this strange girl was still reading from the Four Spiritual Laws she had sat down on the bench next to me to show me. We were on the page with two pictures. One was an image of a seat where self has control and the other was a seat where Christ is in control. I hadn't been thinking about God. It had been many years since I'd convinced my parents to let me stay home and not go with them to church. There'd been too much hypocrisy. I'd been done then and I wasn't interested now.

"Which one do you want for your life?" she finally asked.

I pointed to the image of myself on the throne. "That one."

Her silence and dumbfounded expression didn't surprise me. She'd been expecting me to follow the logic of the four things she'd sat down here to share with me, and I still chose myself. What use was God for, anyways?

"I've got to get to class." I grabbed my backpack off the ground and left her staring at her card in disappointment. The sooner she learned not everybody liked the idea of God in their lives the better.

February, 1972 - Moab, Utah (Four Years Later)

A shooting star went by as I wrapped my sleeping bag tighter around my shoulders. Even in the Utah desert the nights were cold. I couldn't set up a tent on this red rock plateau we'd hiked to today. But this view of the stars was worth it. There wasn't any ambient light for miles and miles around. The view of the Milky Way band was incredible. But out past those stars were more stars and more stars and nothingness in between.

It really was all nothingness. I'd been headed to the Rockies a few weeks ago and realized the only direction in life I had was Interstate 25 right in front of me. There was nothing else. I wasn't going anywhere in life. Just existing. The realization had hit me so hard I turned around, parked my car, and decided to hitchhike with some friends to Utah. Since my life was going nowhere, I thought by hitchhiking I would be going nowhere more slowly! Now here I was half a continent away from Florida where I'd grown up and there wasn't anything here but beautiful stars filling the void of space.

Life was meaningless. Just a big void of meaninglessness. And then there was death. That came to us all. Young or old, rich or poor. We all died and that was it. There's no big grand purpose or anything. It's just us all going our own ways doing what makes us happy.

What made me happy?

An animal howled in the distance. It was wild out here. Untouched land except for the amazing arches and rock formations that defied imagination. Held together by mere gravity and formed by erosion over millennia. I loved architecture. That was something that made me happy. I liked girls. I think I'd like to have a wife someday. Two kids. A dog. And we'd need to have a barbecue in the backyard. That would make me happy. That's what I wanted.

I turned over on my side and closed my eyes to try to sleep. I shouldn't go back to Florida. That was like going backwards in life. One of the guys I'd made friends with out here mentioned he was attending the University of Oregon. It sounded awesome the way he described it, and like a good destination.

Three Months Later - Chase Gardens Plant Nursery - Eugene, Oregon

My orchid plant needed more potting mulch. I grabbed some with my gloved hand and shoved it into the pot. Another one done. On to the next. This is my life right now. Potting orchids until I had lived in Oregon six months and could afford the tuition to University of Oregon and become an architect. I was camping out in a pop up tent in front of my friend's house as a form of temporary residency and had gotten a job here potting orchids.

John, whose station was next to mine, I'd met a few weeks ago. He had three by five index cards plastered all over his workstation with scripture verses on them. He'd told me a bit about Jesus the first few days working here. It was kind of funny because I'd shown up high on mushrooms that first day and he was high on speed. He still liked his Jesus, though. Kept talking my ear off about Him. About a God of love.

John wasn't here today. I was alone out here in the potting room going through dozens of orchids. I grabbed a white one with multiple unopened blooms and a terra-cotta pot to home it in. What if there wasn't nothingness? What if there was more purpose to this life?

I put the orchid and pot down. Why not try?

"Ok God." I looked up at the ceiling. God was out there somewhere, right? "I don't know if you're there, but if you are..." I closed my eyes. Was I doing this right? "Umm…If you're there, I want to know you, know more about you." I guess I could leave it at that?

I turned my focus back to the plant in hand. If God was out there and I mattered at all to Him he could come find me and tell me about himself.

Three Months Later - Liberation House 19th St

"A co-worker of mine, and his mom Bobby asked me a few weeks later if I wanted to go to church with them." I continued my testimony for the inquisitive young lady who'd abruptly sat down and introduced herself to me at dinner.

"No way!" Her eyes got wide. "What about John?"

"I didn't know it at the time but he was backsliding. He didn't invite me to church."

"So then what happened?"

"Well I went to Faith Center. And I was somehow open to it. I was learning about Jesus and I thought I was a pretty good person so you know, like God would want me in his church and I would be a great asset to him. God would want a guy like me. But it wasn't until a few weeks into going that I was at work alone again and it hit me. The weight of my own sin. I was a sinner, and undeserving. God had done an awesome thing in dying for me and I don't know, Mary. I just fell to my knees in the potting debris under my workstation and it hit home."

She had stopped eating her dinner to listen to me. "Wow Russ, that's so cool."

"So, then it gets really good!"

"Ok do go on!" I had her full attention.

"So get this I'm reading my Bible in my friend's backyard smoking a joint because nobody had told me I shouldn't be doing that anymore now that I was a Christian, right?" Mary laughed and I continued. "So I'm reading in first Corinthians where it says you know that your body is a temple of the Holy Spirit and as I took another hit I literally pictured the Holy Spirit choke on the second-hand smoke!"

I laughed with Mary at the memory of that image in my mind. "I took that joint right then and there and snuffed it out in the grass. I was done with that."

"This is such a great story, Russ! Keep going," she encouraged me.

"So then I go to this conference at the Lane County fair fields, and Jerry Cook and Bob Frost are speaking and there's all this pressure to speak in tongues and be filled with the Spirit and I tried so hard. I got prayed for but nothing. Nothing happened! I was devastated! I went home feeling so unworthy that God had taken one look at me and said, "Nope. He doesn't get to be baptized in the Spirit.""

"I hope you don't still think that!" Mary looked concerned.

"Oh no, just wait and hear the rest of it. So, the next day at the conference my buddy Rick comes over and I tell him about what happened and he starts laughing at me and now I'm really confused. He's like, Russ, that's the whole point! None of us are worthy!"

"Mmmm" She nodded in agreement with that nugget of wisdom and I continued.

"So Rick walks over, lays his hand on me and prays with me and I just feel this massive presence overflow from inside me like I can't even describe it very well. Maybe like love and warmth and joy that made me laugh all at once."

"It was the Holy Spirit." Mary nodded with a smile.

"It was the Holy Spirit." I smiled back. "And then, well, I kept going to Faith Center and my friends I met there recommended I join Lib House and now here I am."

"Thanks for sharing your story with me, Russ. I'm glad you're here. I'll let you finish your dinner."

I looked back at my plate that had barely been touched since she'd sat down next to me an hour ago and asked me for my testimony.

"Ya I should probably do that. It was nice meeting you, Mary. I'm glad to be here too."

I waved as she walked away. She was a bold one. They all seemed so kind in one way or another. I'd just been here less than two days and already I was loving the quiet times in the morning. The things Dan Purkey had shared that they tried to work on character wise in the three months people lived in the house were things I needed. Typically they wanted people not working outside jobs and just working on a work crew to help pay for the upkeep of the place. Dan said I was an exception because I already had a job at Chase Gardens, but I was going to try and pull my weight. They'd said they were going raspberry picking tomorrow and then chicken picking the next day. Not sure what the chicken picking thing was but I was curious to find out.

Winter 1972 - Faith Center

I knelt at the altar, taking the time after this mid week service in the emptying sanctuasium to talk to God. I was reevaluating my desire to be an architect now that I'd learned so much being here. I was finding a new love for ministering to people. Just a few weeks ago we'd been interceding over at the women's house for a missions trip and Mary and I had been left in the living room still praying and our prayers had unintentionally turned to thanking the Lord out loud for each other and our friendship and how much we meant to each other and that the Lord had brought us into each other's lives during this time. And then we'd both gotten real quiet at the implications of our confessions. I hadn't looked at her the same since.

I'd graduated from orchids at work to working with roses and kept bringing Mary back the extra ones from work each day. I could tell she knew our relationship had changed too. I was praying about proposing. She could be the one. How would I provide for her though if I didn't go get a degree as an architect?

"Oh God, what should I do?" I prayed again and waited silently for an answer. Some kids ran around playing, while their parents visited or ministered with others, distracting my focus. I was growing in my faith and relationship with the Lord tremendously in this church. Roy Hicks Jr was a phenomenal teacher. He even made time for the theological questions I'd get sometimes like when I'd called him up to ask him about if salvation still counted if you backslide. I'd heard people arguing earlier that day of once saved always saved and the other person disagreed, saying you could lose your salvation. What if you no longer believe in Jesus. Do you lose it even if you did believe it before?

Roy hadn't answered it directly, probably wisely knowing I was still a young believer and figuring all this stuff out. The most important part for me right now was getting to know Jesus. Growing in my relationship with him. Roy had redirected me to the truth. "Ok now Jesus was the son of God right? And you believe he died for your sins and was buried and rose again?" Ya I believed that. Then he'd said, "Ok, well then let's just start from there." Everything always went back to Jesus with him. He was always directing us to that person of Jesus.

You can continue with your education and architecture. The Lord's still small voice brought me back to my question as I still knelt at the altar. *But I have more for you.*

I waited but there was nothing more. This faith was changing my desires. Of course I would want the more the Lord was talking about. I intuitively understood it was a pastoring call. But I also understood there was no bad choice here. He was letting me decide. He knew me better than I knew myself. He knew I loved buildings and design and all the technicality that went with it. He could use me there. He also knew my growing heart for the people around me. This urge to help others find the purpose in their lives I knew now was divinely designed. It wasn't just nothingness out there. There wasn't a void in my life anymore. It was filling up rapidly.

I opened my eyes. I didn't need to hear anymore. I knew what I was going to do.

I got up off my knees and headed out of the gym. I got a ride back to lib house and asked Dan Purkey if I could use the phone to call home. It rang and Mom answered.

"Hey mom, it's Russell."

"Oh goodness honey it's getting late over here is everything ok?"

"Yes, everything is great. I just wanted to call and tell you I'm dropping out of the architect program at U of O and I'm going to explore church ministry as a calling." My mind was made up.

"Oh...." There was silence on the other end of the phone.

"And there's this girl...." I needed to change topics.

"Oh, do tell me more! I can stay up a little longer."

I smiled. My parents might not get my change in careers, but if Mary was the one they'd be thrilled.

And they said to one another, "Did not our heart burn within us while He talked with us on the road, and while He opened the Scriptures to us?" Luke 24:32 NKJV

Russ did not know it at the time, but the "I have more for you" would include marriage, Bible College, and a call towards pastoral ministry...all within one year's time! Mary was indeed "the one." She and Russ were married in July 1973. Russ graduated from LIFE Bible College in 1976, followed by two years on staff at Faith Center. In 1978 Pastor Roy asked Russ and Mary to pray about what "more" God might have in store for them. They felt led to pioneer a new church in Monmouth, Oregon. Eight years later they planted another church in Russ's home town of Boca

Raton, Florida. In 1989, Russ and Mary moved to Colorado and continued in church ministry for an additional twenty years. For the past fourteen years they have been participants in a network of "house churches" in metro Denver. For Russ and Mary, "house church" is more than just their home church. For them it is a return to their roots, which was the authentic Christian community and fellowship they experienced at Lib House and Faith Center when first becoming Jesus people. Russ and Mary recently celebrated their 50th wedding anniversary. They have two children, four granddaughters and one great-grandson.

You can read Mary's story in Chapter 5.

You can read Dan Purkey's story in Volume 1 of Becoming Jesus People.[1]

Lib House, c. 1971. Russ is in the back row, second from the right. Mary is in the front row, second from the right.

---

1. Carissa Gobble and Riley Taylor, "Becoming Jesus People: True Stories of How Love Broke Through In The Jesus People Movement," (GPC Publishing, 2023), 9-12, 149-154.

Chapter 7

The Fired Youth Pastor

Joe's Story

November 1964 - Sweet Home, Oregon

K nock. Knock. Knock.
I opened the front door to see my friend Don Lang.

"Joe, do you want to go to a youth rally tonight at my church?"

My 8th grade self wanted to say no, but I was such a people pleaser that I didn't want to disappoint Don. I wasn't a Christian. I considered myself an atheist so I could do whatever I wanted. And I sure didn't want to go to church on a Saturday night! But I caved.

"Sure.."

"Great! I'll see you at seven!"

"Ok."

If I was going to go do this thing I should grab some other friends to make it less awkward. I knew who I could ask and maybe we'd all go carouse and get into mischief afterwards together. I grabbed my warmest jacket and headed out the door.

That Evening

The preacher had joy.

A joy I hadn't seen before.

A joy I wanted.

Sam Owen was young, fit, and a college student who worked with Campus Crusade for Christ. And everything he shared was making me curious of the happiness he exuded from the pulpit. This wasn't what I thought church would be like. This isn't what I thought Christianity would be like. I'd come here trying to seem cool to my friends, with every intention of going partying afterwards, but now I was intrigued. I wanted whatever this guy had.

"If you'd like to receive Jesus as your Lord and Savior come down to the front." He said.

No one moved.

I froze in my seat.

There was no way I was going down there. Not in front of my friends.

None of them were moving. No one went forward..

The service ended and we headed out. Instead of going out with my friends as we had planned, I headed home, mulling over what I'd heard and seen. I hugged my coat around me a little tighter on the brisk autumn night, crunching red and orange leaves underfoot. About six blocks from home, I stopped. .

"Ok God. I don't know anything about you–only what that guy had to say tonight. But I know what he has, I want. So here I am. Do what you want with me."

Silence.

Not even a light wind whistled in the bare trees that clung to their few remaining leaves but the cold sprung me onward to the physical warmth of my bed that lay up ahead.

August 1973 - Eugene Oregon (Nine Years Later)

"I don't have to tell you you're fired right?" the church elder said with finality, putting into words the gut feeling I had when I'd heard they'd fired pastor Don just yesterday. We'd just sat through Don Smith's last sermon at Westside Church. I was partially to blame. I'd introduced Don to the baptism of the Spirit and spiritual gifts and Don was leading in new ways. The most obvious thing had probably been pastor Don lifting his hands during worship. We'd been going to Faith Center on Wednesday nights for three years even though we were on staff at Westside. I was the youth pastor at Westside. Well, WAS the youth pastor until a minute ago.

"No, I understand." I did—I'd seen it coming. The elder nodded firmly and went on his way. It was actually a relief. This meant we could be a part of Faith Center now. I'd always been outspoken. Even the rest of middle school and high school I'd had this evangelistic passion. The day after that youth revival in 1964 I'd woken up and known I was a Christian. And the only thing I knew Christians did was go to church. So that's what I'd done. I'd gone back to my middle school friend Don's church and my life started changing. I'd instinctively known that my language needed to change, and my days of stealing and mischief were done. Other kids in school started asking me what happened to me and my best response at thirteen years old had been, "I'm religious now."

I smiled as I exited the church for the last time. If my thirteen year old self had only understood that term, "religious." It was exactly the thing pastor Don and I weren't enough of that had gotten us fired this weekend. I had gotten baptized only a few months after my walk home un-eventful salvation experience but getting filled with the Holy Spirit the summer after high school had been a game changer in my relationship with Jesus. If I was bold before I was really bold now. Somehow even back in middle school I'd known I wanted to be a pastor. My eighth grade paper on possible careers was about being a lawyer, a doctor, or a pastor. I knew I'd be a pastor. Then after high school I'd gone on to Northwest Christian College. I had graduated from there recently and had spent my days youth pastoring and in crowded Bible studies at Noel Campbell's house. God was doing something in my generation. Even Time Magazine had published an article about it!

I spotted Don getting in his car in the parking lot and gave him a little knowing wave.

"You too?" He hollered across seven parked vehicles.

I nodded with a smile.

"See you tonight?" He asked, referring to the Sunday evening service at Faith Center.

"Wouldn't miss it!"

On to new adventures I guess. God was still on the throne.

December 1973 - Eugene, Oregon

Ring, ring, ring.

The phone buzzed on the wall in my small studio apartment and I picked up the receiver.

"Is this Joe?"

"Yeah." The voice sounded familiar.

"This is Roy." No wonder it had been familiar. It was Pastor Roy from Faith Center. I now attended all the time, not just evening services.

"Well, hi, Roy."

"I understand that most of our high school students go to your Bible studies."

"Well, yeah, they do."

"I guess that makes you our youth pastor."

What? Was this his way of offering me a staff position at his church? I'd only been going there for four months. We'd never even talked or officially met! This guy was bolder than I thought!

"We'll pay you a hundred bucks a month." He continued.

"Ok." It was the same job I was kind of already doing anyway. "When do I start?"

"You've already started."

"OK, sounds great."

"Great. See ya, Joe."

The line clicked. He'd hung up.

I'd just gotten hired in a sixty second phone call.

The pay wasn't that great but I didn't really care. For the past four months I'd been continuing unofficial youth ministry that had revolved around the Bible study at Noel's house, and in Bible studies at a dozen high school campuses. It wasn't just Faith Center. Students came from churches all over town. It was life giving and I loved seeing these kids catch the same passion I had in high school. I was really excited to be part of what God was doing at Faith Center and experience Roy's leadership. He was leading in the Spirit in very fresh and creative ways. Spiritual gifts were expressed regularly in services. Healings, salvations, deliverance, prophecy, tongues with interpretation. There were probably about eight hundred people crammed into two services in that gymnasium. I laughed at the brevity of the call again.

But really what more words did you need?

Summer 1976 - Faith Center (Three Years Later)

The wedding picture of my stunning brunette bride Laina on my desk was distracting me from planning Sunday's worship set. So many people thought I'd married her just because it meant I got to be Noel Campbell's son-in-law. He was a spiritual father to many in the church and part of the leadership. But really I had fallen in love and somehow gained Noel's approval to have his daughter's hand. Being married had come with a raise to five hundred dollars a month! At that time, Faith Center paid staff based on need. It was an experiment they were trying, not necessarily successfully but I got the heart behind it.

I loved working at Faith Center, and was privileged to work with outstanding young pastors like Alan Ruggles, Ken Klein, Kip Jacob and Steve Overman. We were all working with students from middle school through college age. It was an exciting time of growth and change.

"Hey Joe, you have a minute to chat in the gym?" Roy stood in my office doorway while Cindy Meeks answered the church phone at her desk behind him.

"Of course."

I followed him out of the office suites and down the long sloped hall into the empty sanctuasium. We took two seats on the front row and the space felt strangely smaller than when it was filled to overflowing with people on the weekend.

"Can you explain your message to the youth from last week to me? I think we might be reading Scripture differently on the subject matter." Roy asked.

So that's what this was about. I spotted a Bible on the stage, grabbed it, and flipped open to the passages I'd used last week and talked him through my thoughts.

"We're close enough. It's not a problem." Roy assured me. "But here's the thing. I can't have you teaching something differently than what I'm teaching from up front. When you're leading such a big part of the church, we just can't do that."

I nodded. Unity was important to him.

"So, I'm gonna give you seven days to think about it. Can you adjust your theology on this point? And with good conscience, teach what I'm preaching? And if you can't, then I'm gonna need to let you go."

I understood what Roy was doing and why. And the contrast of this experience from the one at Westside was not lost on me. This man didn't mind that I disagreed with him. He was having this conversation with me in private vs in our offices. He even respected my opinion but he also saw the big picture and that we couldn't have discrepancies in leadership teachings. It was just a different viewpoint, and many Bible scholars taught it the way he did. It was a minor thing yet Roy could see the potential divisiveness it could bring to the congregation. He really cared for the church as a whole.

"I don't need seven days Roy. It's such a small thing. I can adjust that."

"You're sure? I don't want you to if you can't do it in good conscience."

"I could teach that with good conscience. There's a lot of Bible teachers that see it that way. Although lots of them also see it the way I see it, it's totally a secondary issue and I'm happy to adjust to that."

"Thanks Joe." And just like that, we'd resolved the issue.

I wish others could see this. A pastor confronting his staff on a theological issue with respect and understanding that there is legitimate disagreement on things in the Bible but it didn't have to get in the way of unity. We could disagree and still be friends and honor each other. I wondered if this was part of what made this place so different from other churches. I knew personally the simplicity of Roy's teaching had drawn me to the church even before I was a member.

We made our way back to the church offices. Laina was going to get a kick out of the fact that I'd almost gotten myself fired from a second youth pastor job in the span of just six years!

March 1978 - Church Offices - Faith Center (Two Years Later)

I walked through the hallway with orange carpet that covered half the walls of the office suite of rooms clutching my Bible and notebook journal in hand. I recalled a year or so earlier when Roy had met me for lunch and told me I was to be his replacement if he and my father in law didn't make it back from their mission trip to Colombia. He'd handed me an envelope and cassette tape with instructions. Although I'd been honored I'd also been intimidated–scared to death actually! Thankfully it hadn't been necessary. They'd gotten back fine with lots of testimonies to share.

Something Roy frequently told staff, if we complained about how much he was paying us, was that he didn't want us to get comfortable here. He wanted us to go out and plant churches of our own. Some had gone already and had thriving church plants. In December, Roy had told me that I was going to be at Faith Center for a long time. But then on our New Year's Eve watch night service I'd felt the Lord impress on me we were going to be moving and I'd be a lead pastor somewhere. I hadn't felt peace to share that with anyone yet.

Roy almost ran into me as he exited the main office.

"Joe! I was praying for you this week."

That wasn't uncommon. But him telling me he had been praying for me was unusual.

"I think you are supposed to go and pastor your own church."

I smiled a big smile, opened my journal to December 31, and showed it to him.

"I'm three months ahead of you, pastor." I don't think I'd ever been able to say that to him before.

"Well look at that." He smiled at me putting his hand on my shoulder. "God is good."

"Yes he is."

***I have come that you might have life
and have it to the full!***
John 10:10

Joe and his wife Laina moved to Spokane, Washington a month later to pastor a small church of forty people that they named Life Center. At a Foursquare district meeting a few years later with Roy Hicks Sr., Joe and Roy Hicks Jr. had another theological disagreement, yet at the end of the conversation Roy Hicks Sr. pointed out that they could see something differently and still be friends and respect each other and that that is how we should all be in the church. Joe and Laina still serve at Life Center in Spokane. Forty-five years later it has grown to thousands in weekly attendance and their son Michael Wittwer now serves as Lead pastor. Twenty church plants have been started from it. A few years ago Joe reconnected with Sam Owen who had preached the night he got saved. Sam was still under the impression no one had gotten saved that night. Joe got to bring him out on stage one Sunday at Life Center and share with his congregation his testimony and honor the seed he had planted in Joe's life he never knew about. Joe & Laina have five children and ten grandchildren.

Joe says: Roy was such a gift to me–to all of us. I'm so grateful he trusted me and invested in me. I'm forever changed because of it.

Joe and Laina 1978

*Sam Owen on the left and Joe Wittwer on
the right in 2017 at Life Center*

Chapter 8

Pot & Knitting Don't Mix

Molly's Story

June 1973 - Amsterdam, Holland

This was Europe's hippie capital they'd said. Well they weren't wrong. The afros were not in short supply. I stood near the canal watching a boat go down the waterways that riddled the city. There were lots of tourists but I didn't want to stand out as American. They didn't like Americans in Europe. A protest against the policies in the middle east was in full swing a block away. I couldn't understand the Dutch and German words being shouted, but I could see the flags and signs and take a guess. Tensions were hot right now in the middle east. Arab nations threatening a war and an oil embargo.

I knew the feeling these people had. A few years ago I'd been the one marching through the streets of downtown Portland protesting my own government and the pointless Vietnam war. The hatred and distrust of authority was no different here than there. Somehow I'd been under the illusion Europe had it all together.

I'd been wrong. It was just as messed up as it was back home. I spotted a scantily clad woman making out with a man twice her age in the alley to the right and I averted my eyes. I'd curiously taken a trip yesterday down to the famous red light district and that had been an awkward education. The pain of my parents' recent divorce flooded back in. My mom had been a hard woman to live with and had been pretty emotionally abusive to me, as the oldest daughter in the pack of eight siblings. I'd been so glad to get out of there and join my older brother Riley in his hippie life in Eugene. But I think I'd idealized it more than I thought. It had been fun at first but they didn't really seem happy.

It hadn't made me happy either. I was hurting. I loved my dad! He always made me feel safe when he'd walk in the door after work. It was awful watching my mom deteriorate more since the divorce and internally I was wrestling with losing the stability and dependability that my father had been for me before the affair. I had trusted him, he was the rock in my life. The revelation of his infidelity and the subsequent abandonment had shaken my world.

This world as a whole was broken. I was broken. Even my own heart was selfish. In France a week ago I'd left my traveling companion and best friend Mary so she could explore the Louvre another few days and I'd come here. I'd told her I'd meet up with her in Amsterdam but it was a ruse. I'd left a note where she'd find it when she got here. I was abandoning her. Was I any different than my own father? I was really Switzerland bound and leaving my best friend to wander the rest of Europe alone. Then I'd be headed home. It was pointless, searching for something out here in other countries that didn't exist.

"Ding. Ding." A bike bell sounded to my left. I stepped out of the way of an oncoming cyclist and came back to the present. I adjusted my backpack and took in the smell of fresh baked bread from across the street one more time. Well maybe Europe had something going for it. But not at all what I'd expected.

Fall 1973 - Eugene, Oregon

"I'm headed to the grocery store!" I hollered back at my boyfriend as I walked out the front door. An unusual sight on the porch stopped me. There were the words "I love you," spelled out in fall leaves. Tears came to my eyes. Riley and Annamarie had been here again. They were always doing these little sweet things since I'd returned from Europe. They'd changed. Riley had a real joy now. He was different. Annamarie, our younger sister, was also different! We'd never been close growing up but I was feeling drawn to this love they were showing me.

I'd been so mad when I'd first found out they'd become Christians. Not even returning to the Catholic faith of our childhood. I'd followed Riley down here from our home in Portland a few years ago thinking this was the life but I had not even been able to do the hippie thing full on. I still liked my baths and that time I'd gotten high I couldn't see straight to finish my embroidery! It was totally not practical. I didn't get the appeal of it. You couldn't get anything done when you were stoned. I didn't even really like the fact I was living with my boyfriend. We'd told the landlord we were married and I even wore a ring. I knew everyone was doing it. I just felt so embarrassed about it. Riley had gone through a few girlfriends himself but now he was different. He was at this Christian commune place with others like Annamarie.

"You gotta come see what Riley and Annamarie have been up to out here," I yelled into the house.

"I'll see it later." I heard from my boyfriend on the couch. The irony of his disinterest in contrast to the display of love on my front lawn was not lost on me. Every time I ran into my siblings they loved me in some small way. It was filling something in me I couldn't really explain. Like melting ice around my heart or filling an empty bucket starved for real affection.

What day was it?

Sunday!

Where did my siblings say they went to church? It had an interesting name...

Faith Center! That old SDA school had been turned into a church.

I was already dressed and somewhat presentable....

I was going to go.

I was going to go to church!

"Change of plans. I'm headed to church." I yelled back.

"You're what?!"

I stepped back inside and made eye contact with his shocked face.

"I'm going to church."

"They are brainwashing you, Molly!" was his only reply.

I didn't care. I left and hopped on my bike. The church wasn't too far from here.

The parking lot was full but I found a place to stash my bike and walked in. The hall was empty but a sweet melody traveled down it and caressed me like a warm hug. I followed it through double doors that were still open to a large gym full of people and found myself one of the few remaining seats. I wasn't sure what to expect but the singing ended and a short engaging message was delivered while a young preacher sat on a three legged stool. It was different than my memories of Catholic mass. As the sermon ended and people filed out I didn't see my siblings but I was enamored by the love I was witnessing between strangers. Even the preacher was embracing the unshaven, armpit hair, unbathed, shoeless hippies in his congregation. They were welcome here. I was welcome here.

I had chosen church.

I was going to continue choosing church.

"Molly?"

I turned to see a dear friend.

"Nina!"

We embraced. Shocked to have run into each other randomly at a church.

"I didn't know you believed this stuff too Molly!"

"I didn't know you were a Christian Nina! But yes I think I do. It's my first time here."

"Mine too!"

"No way!"

"Where are you living these days?" She looped her hand through my arm.

Shame creeped into my stomach.

Should I tell her?

"I've been at my boyfriend's place but I'm looking for something else." A boldness had come over me from some unknown source.

"We should get a place together!" She was excited.

For the first time in a very long time I felt a warmth in my heart: joy.

This must be what my siblings were experiencing!

Spring 1974 - Eugene, Oregon (The Following Year)

"It needs salt." I put the spoon down on the counter after tasting the chili. "Can you pass me that shaker over there Annamarie?" She found it and handed it to me. I loved having her over to my place. She would tell me all kinds of interesting things. We were making our brother Riley a non-mass produced dinner.

"What was your day like at Lib House?" I asked.

She leaned against the small apartment counter as I tasted the chili again. "Well we had quiet time."

"What's quiet time like?" I asked.

"We spend the first two hours of the morning reading Scripture, praying and journaling just talking to God on our own. Or going over our memory verses."

"Memory verses?"

"Ya like you pick a verse and then go over it again and again like studying for a test until it's stuck in here." She tapped her forehead.

I should do that. I had index cards. I had sticky notes too. And I could carve out more morning time to spend in the Bible. I was hungry for everything. I went to all the Bible studies I could find. There was one on Friday's at Ken Klein's and a college age one at church. And then church on Wednesdays and Sundays.

As soon as I'd said yes to church and the faith that it entailed my life had changed. That joy was still there. Nina and I had moved in together and my boyfriend had been mad. No one had ever said anything to me about living with him or the way I talked or the way I dressed but I had chosen something else. I just started changing, like something inside me wanted to wear modest clothes and clean up my language. It'd been effortless. Instinctive almost. I just ate up everything they told me and taught me in this church. The love I felt with these people was tremendous.

Knock. Knock. Knock.

"I'll get it!" Annamarie dashed to the door.

I smiled. We were always trying to one up each other when it came to Riley. He'd sort of filled in a fatherly family leadership role for those of us that were believers now. Funny how we could not be very close growing up and then all bond over a new found love for Jesus.

Annamarie let Riley in and enjoyed a huge hug from him.

"Smells amazing Molly!" he said as he slipped off his coat.

"It's ready! Go grab a seat!" I shouted through the kitchen opening.

God was transforming me and my family right before my very eyes.

Summer 1975 - Noel Campbell's Bible Study - Eugene, Oregon (One Year Later)

"Well what is Jesus telling you to do about it Molly?" Noel Campbell asked me. I'd come early to Bible study to help with the food and to run some private questions by Noel. I didn't like it when he didn't give me straight answers. At least pointing me back to Jesus was better than his silence. Silence meant he didn't approve.

Noel had become like a spiritual dad to me. In those first few weeks of choosing church over my old life I'd wrestled with my boyfriend relationship and letting him go. The three bubbly sisters in the same apartment complex had brought me sobbing to Noel's house and I'd fallen at his feet a total emotional wreck. He had this fatherly presence that had met me where I was with wisdom and counsel. But I wasn't that baby Christian anymore and now he was challenging me to find some of my answers directly from Jesus. I should take it as a compliment. I was growing up spiritually.

"Hey everybody!" Stephie Beckett walked in the door bringing me back from my recollections. "I've got the bread!" She held up some white loaves.

"Is that wonder bread?!" I asked.

"Of course! Wonder bread uses that new enriched flour that's so great for our bodies!" Stephie shut the door behind her.

"But it takes out all the real nutrients!"

She stared at me with incredulity. "Molly, we are going to feed these hungry souls with good bread not just for their spirits but also their bodies."

Noel interjected, "Girls! We can let people choose for themselves. I've got some whole wheat in the cupboard."

I kept my mouth shut and Stephie walked to the kitchen to prep. What had I been asking Noel about? It wasn't coming back to me but I had another question.

"Do you think I should go back to college?"

He thought for a moment. "I think that would be a good question to ask your father about."

He was right. Things had gotten better between Dad and me in the past few years. I loved talking with him, although it had to stay practical. He wasn't interested in his kids' new found Protestant faith. But someday I knew he would be. I'd give him a call and talk to him about college later.

The door opened again and Christina O'Grady entered. "Molly! I was hoping I'd see you today!" She came and sat next to me on the couch opposite of Noel. "They are going to need a new shepherdess for a few months at one of the church's discipleship houses, House of Glory. Roy asked me to see if you would pray about it. He thinks you'd be perfect for the role."

I looked over at Noel and saw him smiling. I was probably a good fit, especially if it was temporary. I'd been sharing my new faith with everyone around me. It was like an instinct to pass on what I was learning to other young ladies finding their way. Just like Noel was being a spiritual Father to me I guess I was learning how to be a spiritual mother. It was humbling to know the pastor saw this in me and thought I'd be good for the job.

"Wow. Yes I'll definitely pray about it."

The door opened yet again and I knew my one on one time was up. A group of guys walked in. They were new. But they'd been coming a couple times now and I loved watching how Jesus was bringing them the same love and forgiveness I'd come to know. It was astoundingly merciful for God to have seen me in my brokenness and wandering and let His love work through my siblings those few years ago. Here I was, now surrounded with love and community and growing continually. There was real joy here. We didn't all agree on the small things like bread but the important things like Christ's love knit us together like a family.

A family you'd see nowhere else.

"Molly, will you come help in the kitchen?" Stephie asked sweetly, peeking her head around the kitchen door frame. The confrontation of a moment ago had been forgotten.

"Yes!" I jumped up from the couch to help.

> **It was going to be a great Bible study no matter what the bread tasted like.**
> *You will make known to me the way of life; In Your presence is fullness of joy; In Your right hand there are pleasures forever.*
> **Psalms 16:11 NASB**

Fifty years later Molly restored the relationship with Mary who she had abandoned in Europe. Molly also led her ex-boyfriend to the Lord, though they did not end up getting back together. Molly has gone on to be not only a natural mother of five children but now also a grandmother of ten. She did go back to school and complete her degree. She has tutored many students over the years and is claimed as a spiritual mother by dozens of women. She has served in various capacities in churches in the Portland area and currently spends her time helping her family and nurturing her grandchildren. A few years ago she was able to lead her dad's wife to the Lord on her deathbed, her dad gave his life to Jesus a few months later. She continues to be a nurturing and encouraging spiritual mother and grandmother to many. She currently lives in Oregon City tending her flower farm. She blessed two hundred people with bouquets from it last year and aims to double that this upcoming year.

Riley, Annamarie, Stephie and Christina's stories can be found in Becoming Jesus People Volume 1.[1]

---

1. Carissa Gobble and Riley Taylor, "Becoming Jesus People:True Stories of How Love Broke Through In The Jesus People Movement," (GPC Publishing, 2023), 35-44, 103-108,89-96, 53-62.

Molly

Chapter 9

What Does Jesus Say?

Cheri's Story

1973 - Eugene, Oregon

"I ntroduce yourself to the person next to you," the church college group leader instructed. I turned to the blond blue eyed girl beside me.

"Hi, I'm Cheri," I offered.

"I'm Stephanie." My jaw dropped.

"Stephanie Skeie?" I asked.

"Yes! Are you the Cheri I was supposed to meet here today!"

"Yes!" I was dumbfounded. Of all the odds the person I'd sat next to was the person I was here to meet! I'd been given no description of her, just a name from my co-worker Ella who'd been hearing me complain how I had no Christian friends in this big city. I was a country girl from a small town, Lorane, still getting used to the culture shock of so many people everywhere all the time. I knew I needed to make some changes in my life. I needed Christian friends to be positive influences. I'd had enough of the not so good influences. Ella had told me I needed to meet a girl from her church and she'd set it up for us to both come to this college group.

This had to be a God setup!

We both laughed at the non-coincidence of it all..

I liked her already.

"Cheri, do you want to go with me to check out this church called Faith Center I keep hearing about after this group?" Stephanie asked as we sat down.

"Sure!"

A Few Hours Later - Faith Center

A strange language erupted from a young man to my right and the entire congregation turned to stare at him. What was that? This was a very interesting place Stephanie had brought us too. She'd heard great things, but this was a little weird. I was used to a very traditional style of church.

"This is not the right time brother," the pastor, Roy Hicks Jr., addressed the situation from the pulpit. The man stopped. "Hold that thought and if the Lord tells me that there's an appropriate time, I will let you speak." The congregations' focus returned to the pastor's message. As did my own. Although I'd never been in one, I'd heard pentecostal churches were typically known for their wild, out of control, disordered manifestations of the Holy Spirit. But here it seemed maybe it was different. There was order and I felt safe with a leader steering the flow of whatever was happening here. It didn't feel chaotic.

"If you see your target way out in front of you and for every step towards it you take one little step sideways, over time, you're going to miss the mark." Roy continued his message and his metaphor hit home in my own past choices. Give a little here. Ignore my conscience a little there.

"But God is bigger than our choices and mistakes. We can end up on the wrong path and He can still put a big detour or blockade in front of us to steer us back on course." He paused in the middle of the little circular stage at the end of the gym. "I want us to end with a song. Will you stand?"

The shuffle of seats and sneakers on the green carpeted gym floor answered the pastor's request. "Grab your neighbor's hand and look them in the eye. Don't get weird about it. This is your brother or sister here." The room erupted in laughter diffusing some of the awkwardness. I was fine. I held Stephanie's hand. Even though we'd just met mere hours ago she wasn't a stranger. The pastor sat down at the piano and started to play a simple melody. "Sing this with me." This was new. I hadn't really seen a pastor lead his own worship before.

"Oh I love you with the love of the Lord. Yes I love you with the love of the Lord.....I can see in you, the glory of our King, and I love you with the love of the Lord." Tears came to my eyes as we finished. I felt connected, loved, and inspired. It was such a simple song but I saw the same hunger in the people in this place for more of God that I too was craving. This is what I had been desiring. The hunger and thirst for God and his Word.

The Next Day - Local Coffee Shop

The potent comforting smell of french roast wrapped around me as Stephanie Skeie finished sharing her testimony from her time in Hawaii with Teen Challenge. I took another sip of my mocha and couldn't believe the instant connection I'd felt with this woman. I smiled, remembering our mutual shock when we'd happened to sit next to each other in that crowded room yesterday.

"That's amazing Stephanie!"

"Please call me Stephie, everyone does. What's your story Cheri?"

"Well... it's not quite as exciting as yours. I was twelve and I remember there was a visiting evangelist, Vern Gomez. My mom and I went to all his nightly meetings at our church. His wife would create these chalk drawings as he shared the gospel and then would shine a black light on the drawings and parts of the picture would be illuminated so it brought out the things we never noticed before. I was enthralled by it all and when my pastor gave an altar call that next Sunday, I grabbed my friend's hand, told her she needed to be saved too, and drug her to the front with me." I took another sip of my coffee. "That's about all there is to it. I chose to believe in the Lord God. Who he was and what he had done for me and to commit my life to him that day.."

"I love that Cheri! I wish I'd had a longer relationship with Jesus like you!"

"I wouldn't say it was a very close relationship at first." I avoided her gaze and continued. "As a teen, I convinced myself I would be safe going with my friends to their parties. "I knew better, I was a Christian, I thought I could even influence them. But I'm sure you can imagine how that went." I rolled my eyes and Stephie chuckled.

"Isn't it great how Jesus just wipes the slate clean though?" Stephanie's bubbly personality was so contagious, I was drawn to her like a magnet. I needed a kindred spirit. Someone to grow in my faith with; and God had provided one. What an answer to my prayers.

A Year Later - Noel Campbell's House

Noel put his cup of coffee down, still intently reading his Bible while I took another sip of mine. He let us young folk join him for his quiet time and coffee in the morning if we wanted to. A few days ago he'd gotten adventurous and dragged me to the hospital with him and we'd prayed for the sick people there. He just lived out his convictions like that. His wedding ring glistened in the early morning rays of sunshine. His wife had died of cancer many years ago and he had never taken it off. He'd just switched pouring out his love on his wife to pouring it out on all us young new Christians. Every week there could be up to 25 kids piled into his living room for Bible study. He was a spiritual father to so many of us. I'd come with a question of my own this morning to which he'd given me the, "Go home and pray! What is Jesus telling you?" redirection.

I couldn't take the silence anymore, "Would you please just tell me what I should do? You're a man of God and have wisdom!"

Noel looked up from his Bible and smiled at me. Words came out of his lips but I couldn't hear him. I tapped my deaf ear and repositioned myself so my good ear would be towards him. "Can you repeat that?" He knew I'd lost hearing and gotten a hole in my eardrum when I was a child from scarlet fever. Six surgeries later, there was no success and I still couldn't hear out of that ear.

"What are you hearing, Cheri?" he repeated.

Ugh the same redirected question. "Well.... I was reading in Psalms today. Psalm 91. You know the part where it says we may observe the calamity of the wicked with our eyes, but the evil will not come near us? That the Lord is our refuge and will guard you in all your ways.

He nodded.

"Maybe He's telling me not to worry about it. I see the trouble and I want to do something about it but He's got me covered?"

"That sounds like a good plan Cheri. Sounds like the Lord to me." He turned back to his Bible and took another sip of coffee. I wished he'd just give me the answers but I knew he was being a good spiritual dad, training me to be dependent on the Lord instead of him. And it was slowly working. There was a peace that accompanied that scripture I'd just read. Peace and application to my inner musings. Maybe this is how it was supposed to work. This community thing. As much as I loved the connection and fellowship, it was also a way for us to nudge each other towards Jesus. To collectively keep growing and keep our eyes on God. My twelve year old faith was being transformed into more of a relationship with God. It wasn't always easy, but it was exactly what I needed.

Six Month Later - Eugene, OR

My roommate Stephie was studying with her lab partner for a final coming up but all I could see were her scaly eczema covered eyelids. I'd just come from a Happy Hunters meeting where this visiting couple had shared so many testimonies of healing and then prayed over all of us to have an opportunity to let God use us to encounter someone else that needed prayer. Well I hadn't even thought of Stephie but she had this skin issue she was dealing with.

"Stephie, I have to pray over you!" I walked up to her and her study partner.

"Well, ok, Cheri." She put down her textbook.

"We need to trust God." I put my hands on her eyes with residual boldness from the meeting I'd just been in. "Jesus, please bring your healing touch to Stephie's eyes. We pray and ask in your name Jesus."

I lifted my hand away and blinked a few times. Was I seeing things?

The redness was gone! The flaky skin was falling off and her eyelids were like new!

I looked at Stephie's study partner and saw her shocked eyes confirming I wasn't imagining things.

"What?" asked the oblivious Stephanie to her own healing.

"Look in the mirror Steph."

She got up and walked over and her jaw dropped at her own eczema free reflection.

"Thank you Jesus!" I ran over and hugged her. "Jesus healed you, Steph!"

Stephie's study partner was still speechless, surrounded by textbooks. Tears were starting to form in Stephanie's eyes. "Yes. Yes he did." She hugged me back.

I'd never seen a real live miracle! Let alone one I'd been able to pray for!

This sold out, surrendered Christian life was more amazing than I could've ever imagined. It was full of imperfect people loving a perfect God. I was not the same person I was a few years ago and I had Jesus and this fellowship of other believers cheering me on to thank for it. Trying to walk out my faith on my own hadn't gone so well, but here I was loved and accepted. Here I was learning and growing in my faith. Here I had friends and that twelve year old salvation experience was transforming into a real living, breathing, walk of faith and trust with Jesus. To be forgiven and cleansed by the blood of Jesus and in relationship with God, my Father and my redeeming Savior, Jesus. How could anyone not want this?!

Stephie and I turned to her study partner and said almost simultaneously, "Do you know Jesus?"

For I am confident of this very thing,
that He who began a good work in you
will perfect it until the day of Christ
Jesus **Philippians 1:6**

Be anxious for nothing, but in every-
thing by prayer and supplication with
thanksgiving, let your requests be
made known to God. And the peace of
God, which surpasses all comprehen-
sion, will guard your hearts and your
minds in Christ Jesus.
Philippians 4:1

Cheri continued to attend Faith Center for another 30 years. In 1978 she married Don Wilson. The miraculous continued to follow her life. In 2012 she found out from her ear doctor she'd been to since she was a child that she had a new eardrum and was able to use a hearing aid to hear. There was no scientific explanation for it. It was a miracle. She also saw God heal her granddaughter from a platelet disease as a baby. That granddaughter is fourteen years old now and walks in wholeness. Cheri enjoys mentoring young mothers and serving where the Lord leads. She and her husband have four children and four grandchildren. She lives in Sisters, Oregon with her husband Don and they attend Sisters Community Church.

You can read Stephanie's story in Becoming Jesus People Volume 1.[1]

*Cheri with a friend's child,
1977.*

*Cheri and her husband
Don, 1980.*

1. Carissa Gobble and Riley Taylor, "Becoming Jesus People:True Stories of How Love Broke Through In The Jesus People Movement," (GPC Publishing, 2023), 89-96.

Chapter 10

Can't Be a Christian Anymore

Cindy's Story

1969 - Eugene Police Station

I sat on a bench in the holding room after the officer called my mom to come get me. I'd snuck out at night with some friends, and they had stolen a car. My older sister was the good kid, responsible. I was the troublemaker of the five siblings. My mother was solo parenting since Dad had sent us back to Oregon to live with my aunt and uncle three years earlier. The rejection still stung. Although typically preoccupied with work, Dad had been in my life for my first twelve years. Then he'd gotten fed up with us all. I don't think he had planned on having five kids. My mom joked that every time he hung his pants up on the bedpost she'd gotten pregnant. I had tried to please him the best I knew how. But even at five years old he'd called me an idiot. Still, part of me loved him.

Mom had stopped taking us to Catholic mass when I was eight years old. Probably because we moved so much for Dad's work. I'd been in ten different schools already. Nothing really felt like home. As much as I wanted to please God when I was younger, it quickly had become apparent it was impossible. Much like my relationship with my dad. I had given up. Not attending mass was a mortal sin. If I couldn't do that then what was the point of even trying anymore?

"Cindy Brown!" The officer motioned me over to the doorway.

"Your Uncle Don and Aunt Phyll are here to take you home."

My hardened heart somehow got harder. Mom hadn't come. I really was her worst nightmare. She'd started drinking recently and I was probably the cause of it. The black sheep of the family. I hung my head as I followed the officer towards my impending doom. At least I only had to go back to our house with Mom and my siblings. The first year we'd been in Eugene we'd all crammed into my Aunt and Uncle's three bedroom house along with their three kids. Hopefully the cousins wouldn't hear about this. But really, what did it matter anyways? I was making myself worthless and unlovable to them all. I pushed the shame into any corner of my soul still left empty and braced for the barrage of reprimands.

June 1972 - Faith Center - Eugene, Oregon (Three Years Later)

The short guy pacing the stage was talking about adoption again and blowing my mind. Not the literal kind of adoption but the God being like a Father to us sort. I'd heard him talk about this a year ago when Jan Titus and Laketa Morse had brought me to this church when it'd been in a small chapel on 18th street. Now they were in a gym with basketball hoops still hanging from the rafters, arranged chairs for pews on the marked floor and my heart was connecting with his words in a way it hadn't a year ago. Jan sat next to me. I'd called her up and asked her to take me back to this church and she'd obliged. She was a good friend. She cared. The boyfriends, though I'd thought they loved me and would fill the void in my heart for care and worth, turned out to just be using me. One had even led to an unexpected pregnancy.

My mom had held my hand through the resulting abortion. In some ways that's what had woken me up. My lifestyle was accumulating consequences I hadn't anticipated. My poor mother was doing her best, in spite of her own personal struggles. She loved us all so much. I knew abortion was another sin on my rapidly growing list of offenses in God's eyes. Yet this message of repentance, forgiveness and God welcoming us in like a father drew me in like water to a parched throat.

Could all this really be true? Could God really love me in all my imperfections? After all my bad choices? After all the chaos I'd caused people? Did it all really not dissuade him from sacrificing His son for me? Something in this place felt so organic and real, not just hype or ritual. And the message was sparking something in my heart I hadn't felt in years.

Hope.

"I'd like everyone to close their eyes. If you want to respond to Jesus and give him your life and be adopted into the family of God by a loving Father, I want you to raise your hand. This isn't about your neighbor, it's about you and a Father. You and His son Jesus. Will you accept this gift none of us deserve?" With my closed eyes I felt my hand go up. I was going to give this a try. I knew I had to change something. Why not try this? I had nothing to lose. I followed along with the pastor's salvation prayer under my breath and a forgiveness flooded me. The sins I'd accumulated seemed to lift off in a moment.

"Praise God!" The whole gymnasium cheered for their new brothers and sisters. Even though there was nothing to identify us with, Jan gave me a side hug and I knew she could tell. I was different now. The past life was done. I was going to try to please God again.

January 1973 - House of Glory - Eugene, Oregon (Six Months Later)

I shivered, huddled around the open oven on the floor of the kitchen with the other seven female residents during our house devotions. Linda Hume, our house shepherdess, was leading us in a reading of the Psalms. The irony of praising God in all circumstances was not lost on us. The basement had flooded. There was no heat in the house except what we could get the kitchen oven to put out and we could see our own breath in the frigid air every time we read another verse.

I couldn't complain though. At least we weren't chicken picking like the people at Liberation House did. Sometimes the Lib Housers would come to our Bible studies, sometimes us to theirs. But we'd only ever taken them up on their invitation to go chicken picking once. And I would sit in a freezing kitchen over doing that again any day!

Knock. Knock. Knock.

Linda got up to open the back door and found Roy, our pastor, standing there in his winter coat. Bible in his gloved hands. "Hey ladies, can I join you for devotions?"

Was he serious?

We all stared up at him in shock from our bundled spots on the floor.

"Of course." Linda welcomed him in and sealed the door behind him to keep out the unwanted winter.

We all shuffled a bit to make room for him and Linda jumped back into the passage. I tried to focus but the fact that the pastor would come to visit one of his church's discipleship houses when it was an ice cube intimidated me for some reason. Is this what pastors did in Protestant churches? They cared about the trivial things? The lack of heat?

I had really thrived within the structure of this new Christian life. Multiple church services a week. Daily devotions. Friends that weren't pulling me in different directions. My mom wasn't too thrilled when she'd found out I'd gotten baptized back in October but I do think she was relieved to have me out of the house finally. Not giving her mischievous grief anymore. Just spiritual grief. But it didn't matter. I belonged here now. I really felt like I finally was part of something. Roy had asked me if I wanted the open spot in this discipleship house a few months ago and I'd jumped on the chance to grow with other women in this new relationship with Jesus. It had been an amazing journey except of course for the whole flooded basement and no heat in the dead of winter thing today.

Knock. Knock. Knock.

Roy got up this time and answered it.

"I heard there's a furnace that needs fixing and some plumbing work, too?" One of the church elders held up a massive black metal tool box in the doorway.

We all cheered as Roy shut the door and Linda showed the men down to the basement. Some of my walls were slowly melting away and revealing this idea of men being helpful, caring, and trustworthy. Loving us like family.. These two guys had heard of our need and made it their problem to come fix. How they'd heard about it I didn't know but something in my heart was softening. I really truly did belong here.

Spring 1976 - The Garden House - Eugene, Oregon (Three Years Later)

My old ways of thinking were bubbling up again, I didn't think I could do this Christian life anymore. I couldn't please God. Louise gently ran her brush through my thick hair as I sat on her bed and debated sharing some of my inner turmoil. I had taken over for Linda as house shepherdess back in the House of Praise for two years. I had no leadership skills, I didn't know why they thought I'd be any good at it. I was thankful to not be in that role anymore and instead here at this house with Louise as the lead. But I was also teaching Sunday school to a class of fifty kids each week and this past week it had been ninety! Jack Hayford had been visiting so it had drawn an even bigger crowd. I really did love teaching Sunday school, even though it felt like I didn't know what I was doing. I never felt prepared, yet I'd show up week after week and hear this still small voice telling me in my spirit, "*You are loved, you are useful, you are mine*".

Yet here I was with anxiety to the point I plastered on fake smiles so no one would know my inner critic and depression were growing leaps and bounds daily. I kept listening to the other voice in my head that sometimes sounded like my father. "You're an idiot." I never felt qualified for any of these roles and jobs I was doing in this church. I didn't see how I could move forward any further. I just couldn't do it anymore. But I knew I did NOT want to go back to the way I was before. If there was no forward and no backward what else was there? Was this the end?

Maybe I should end it.

"Ow!' I grabbed my head where Louise had pulled a little too hard on a tangle.

"Sorry!" She apologized.

The truth leaked out of me, "Louise. I don't think I can keep being a Christian."

She put down the brush and was silent.

I turned to face her. A little afraid I'd see judgment in her countenance towards me after my deep internal turmoil had been revealed. But no. All I saw was calm, poised, grace as if this was the most ordinary thing to say in the world.

"You're too hard on yourself, Cindy."

Was I?

She gave my hand a squeeze and returned my brush.

I got up off the bed in a daze and went back to my own room, flopping myself down on the bed. My Bible still lay there from my morning devotion time open to the book of Psalms. I flipped through a few pages and stopped at Psalms 18.

> He sent from above, He took me; He drew
> me out of many waters. He delivered me
> from my strong enemy, From those who
> hated me, For they were too strong for

me. They confronted me in the day of
my calamity, But the Lord was my support. He also brought me out into a broad
place; He delivered me because
He delighted in me.[1]

Tears began to well up. A picture in my mind formed of God swooping down from heaven to pick me up out of the waves of despair, meeting me and coming to my rescue even in the darkest parts of my psyche and heart because of His mercy. Not because of my perfection. He would deliver me because He was delighted in me.

He delighted in me.

I couldn't hold them back any more. The dam burst and tears dripped onto the pages as the concept of mercy became real. Even though I wasn't perfect. Even though I wasn't who I thought I should be at this point in life, He loved me just as I was. He really had forgiven me. He was really with me. He wouldn't forsake me. And that meant I could make friends with people like Louise based on transparent honesty and not just a fake 'everything is ok' persona. Louise hadn't thought me weird. She'd just thought I might need to change how I viewed myself.

Maybe I really was too hard on myself.

Maybe if I changed the way I was thinking, my feelings would follow.

I grabbed a pen off my nightstand and underlined those verses, dog-earring the page so I could return to it again in the morning and remind myself what it said. If I was going to keep going with this Christian life I needed words like this. And I needed friends and a community to support me.

---

1. Psalms 18:16-19 NKJV

December 1977 - Fireside Room - Faith Center
(The Following Year)

Crash! Glass shattered across the table from the broken Christmas ornament
Lynn Stanchfield had just dropped. "I didn't like that one anyways" she said as
Laurie Aldrich, Vickie Becker and I all clung a little tighter to our own ornaments
and laughed. We were decorating for the staff Christmas party. Transforming this
basement room into something festive. We just had a few finishing touches to put
up. I placed my ornament on a gold garland that we'd strung from the fireplace to
the window and then went over to find a broom to help Lynn clean up the mess.

The north door to the room opened and we heard steps descend the U-shaped
creaky stairs. Roy's wide eyes appeared at the bottom as he took in the scene and
we all froze. Would he be ok with it? We really had transformed it into some sort
of Bon Marché department store festive feel. We were just missing Bing Crosby
singing White Christmas over a mall intercom to complete the look.

Roy didn't intimidate me like he used to. My insecurity and fear of the first few
years at Faith Center had really turned around after that day with Louise. I'd
even been greeted by him in the lobby one time while covering a secretarial shift
with an innocent fatherly kiss on my cheek. And it had sort of melted a little
more of my heart, still starved for love from my own father. I wasn't as afraid or
untrusting as I had been. I wasn't so critical of myself any more. Changing the
way I thought about me had flushed the depression away. I was learning about
this relationship with Jesus and Father God that was satisfying a deep longing in
my soul I never knew existed, and this community around me was the perfect
incubating environment.

Roy inhaled deeply and brought me back to the present moment. He didn't
always like surprises. The "Happy Forty Shorty" billboard sign for his birthday
hadn't gone over so well. I held my breath.

"It looks like the daughters of Babylon have been in here." He let out a little laugh
at last and we all joined him with nervous giggles. It may have been a bit over the

top, it's true. All the baubles and bangles and a variety of colors dominated by green and red. Every corner of the room had been made over by one of us with the Christmas festive spirit. Roy walked through the room and out the other door with no other words or comments. Lynn gave a little shrug as we all let out a sigh of relief that the pastor hadn't objected.

I handed Laurie the broom as Vickie stacked the last few empty decor boxes up so we could finish up and then get ready for the party later. I was still amazed that Vickie had asked me to come on staff a year ago as Sunday School support after she'd seen how I ran my class. I'd only been a Christian a few years. But the church was growing so fast leaders and helpers were needed every which way you looked. It was like a family though. We looked out for each other. I felt connected to these ladies and this community. I belonged here. I could recognize and receive the love that surrounded me now like I'd never been able to do before.

You are loved. You are useful. You are mine.

That still small voice filtered through my mind again and made my heart skip a beat.

Nothing compared to the relationship I was developing with Jesus.

He'd changed everything.

I was forever changed.

> **Be strong and courageous. Do not fear**
> **or be in dread, for it is the Lord your**
> **God who goes with you. He will not**
> **leave you or forsake you.**
> **Deuteronomy 31:6-8**

Cindy attended Faith Center for thirteen years and served on staff for six years. She returned to school and became a dental hygienist, now retired after twenty-five years. Cindy married Rick Smith in 1977. Though their marriage did not last, they worked hard to remain friendly as their children Melody and Amanda grew up. Rick died in hospice in Cindy and her second husband Mike's home in 2018. She and Mike have six kids between them and thirteen collective grandchildren. They attend Springfield Faith Center which was a plant from the original Faith Center in 1981. She enjoys the women's ministries and continues as a volunteer in Sunday School and in various other ways. She co-leads a Genesis class as well. Her mother had treatment in Serenity Lane in 1981 and remained sober the rest of her life. A few years ago Cindy was able to reconnect with her father during the last few weeks of his life, bringing healing and closure to their relationship. She has continued to grow in her relationship with Jesus and renew her mind over the past decades to where anxiety is no longer a stronghold in her life. She says that if it weren't for meeting Jesus she would likely be insane or no longer living. She and her husband currently reside in Springfield, Oregon.

Mike Hume, Linda Hume's husband, is mentioned in David's story in Becoming Jesus People Volume 1. You can read Louise's testimony also in Volume 1.[2]

House of Glory Discipleship House

---

2. Carissa Gobble and Riley Taylor, "Becoming Jesus People:True Stories of How Love Broke Through In The Jesus People Movement," (GPC Publishing, 2023), 127-132, 13-18.

Cindy in the middle with friends.

Faith Center Sunday School Staff. Cindy is in the back row, third from the left.

Chapter 11

Roy's Story Part 2

1970 - Faith Center 18th st - Eugene, OR

"Ready to go check out another facility with me while you're here?" I asked my dad and brother Jim who were visiting this weekend. The church had been growing rapidly and I knew we were going to need a bigger space at some point. I wanted to be prepared.

"Yep," Dad responded as Jim nodded and we made our way to the car.

There was an apartment property for sale not too far away and we got out of the car to look at it.

"I was thinking Kay and I could live in one of the apartments and then we could remodel the rest into a sanctuary and sunday school rooms, an office, etc." I pointed at the long building.

"What about parking and bathrooms though?" Dad asked contemplatively.

I started counting the spaces as we entered the building to look at the inside.

"This is going to be too small Roy," Dad said after we'd walked through it. I trusted Dad's opinion on this. This place was twice the size of the little chapel we were in now but we had doubled our numbers in a matter of weeks and now just three months later, it was getting cramped. Also the frogs under the floorboards in the Sunday school rooms were an interesting addition to the chorus of praise we would lift up each week, and the roof had leaks. It was not uncommon for people to bring umbrellas to service to keep dry.

"Ok, well, there is another building," I said as we filed back into the car. I turned on the ignition and backed out of the parking lot and headed towards 13th and Polk street.

We arrived at the Seventh Day Adventist school building. It had a quonset hut shaped roof over the gym. It felt massive. How had I ended up looking at a property this size? The ten wooden pews on each side of the aisle at our current place were now packed and overflowing. What happened to our small church of fifty people God?

We got out and looked around. "This is it Roy." Dad said confidently. "This will work."

Dad saw potential in things others didn't. I guess we could make it work. It would definitely take the churchy feel out of our gatherings if we met in a gym. The thought of filling it was a bit intimidating though. God seemed to have other plans than my idealized small church of a handful of people to love Jesus and each other with. In my heart I recognized that old familiar pull again to a life outside the public ministry.

But no.

I chose this.

I had said yes.

My yes meant yes. He would sustain us. He would provide.

You can reach the whole world through the local church....

That still small voice echoed in my heart bringing the reassuring presence of Jesus with it.

The Next Day

"When we all get to heaven, what a day..." The lyrics from our last closing hymn that Pauline had pounded out on the piano in true pentecostal style at the end of service still rang in my ears as I walked up to a newer member of our congregation. "Brenda, do you play the piano?" I asked the sweet woman who'd been coming with her fiancé Paul for the past five weeks to our small but rapidly growing pastorate.

"Well, yes, classically. I've been classically trained." She replied.

"Do you play by ear at all?" I prodded further.

Her stance stiffened nervously with her reply. "Not a bit, I just read music."

"Well, I want you to pray about it. I think you're supposed to become our church pianist."

Now I could tell she was really nervous, "But that just can't be, I cannot even play Jesus Loves Me by ear!"

I was sure though. We needed to pivot our worship and be able to flow as the Spirit led. I did this already, feeling inspired with new lyrics, typically something in the Psalms I'd recently read I'd lead the congregation in a praise response to Jesus. Recently a melody on my heart kept coming up out of Psalms 18. I'd been reading it in my office and inspiration had hit. I just walked over and sat down at the piano tinkering with a melody from King David's own words.

Praise the name of Jesus.
Praise the name of Jesus.

My dad wasn't a fan of repeating choruses like that in church, and would tell me it, too. I respected him but we didn't agree on everything. I was grateful for the foundation he'd given me as a child and sometimes rebellious teen. I recalled the time he'd given me five dollars when I was sixteen because I could recite the whole chapter of Romans eight by memory. I smiled as I remembered Jim memorizing Psalms chapter one and reciting it to dad with no such luck. The discrepancy of six verses to thirty-nine verses probably was the reason. We'd had a solid foundation in the word growing up. Listening for the direction of the Holy Spirit in the worship times of service wasn't something I'd grown up learning.

But music and flowing with it as the Spirit led felt natural to me. Almost as if I was nudged by the Lord sometimes. But it required someone to be able to play with me on the piano by ear. Brenda's dad had mentioned she played, and I'd mentioned it to Pauline, who to her credit could have been offended by me asking to replace her, yet she went right along with the idea. The woman amazed me and I was grateful we had people like her in our congregation as mother figures to our rapidly growing younger demographic. "I cannot do this," Brenda reiterated insecurely.

I could be wrong but Brenda held potential I didn't think she realized yet. I put my hand on her shoulder, "Well Brenda, with God all things are possible and I'm praying. You just pray and see if the Lord has something to say to you about that."

We smiled at each other and I left it at that and walked over to Dad, Mom and my brother Jim, who had been visiting today. I had given Dad the pulpit this morning and he'd given one of his one hundred and fifty sermons on faith as he liked to say. Jim had found the seating dynamic just as amazing as I had when I'd pulled the curtain back that separated the living space from the sanctuary and showed him this hippie girl with hair to the floor sitting right next to a straight woman in a pencil skirt, pearl necklace and hat. Jesus made this kind of thing possible. Some had not adjusted to the changes we were making, and the people that were showing up. We'd lost a few of those original fifty people. But in no other place would you find two polar opposites choosing a seat next to one another.

I shook hands and smiled at the lingering members of the congregation. These people were really becoming in love with Jesus. The person of Jesus, not just the concept. A lot of what I felt the Lord leading me to teach on these days was the simple gospel. The dailiness of walking out a relationship with Jesus. It was astounding how many were coming, knowing they could come just as they were. There had been the biggest crowd yet, today. Apparently another church in the city had told all its members to leave and come here instead. I was hoping the school would work out eventually that we had looked at yesterday, but we were probably going to have to do something temporarily here until it was ready.

"Jim, do you think we could knock out this wall here and make more space so people aren't outside?" I asked my brother.

He looked at the wall I was pointing to.

"I don't see why not."

If it was God's will for us to grow He would have to help us make the space work.

Late Spring 1972 - Eugene, OR (Two Years Later)

The warm summer wind across my face was invigorating. I loved the outdoors. I sped down 18th street on my bicycle kicking up last night's rain puddles in my wake and then screeched to a halt in front of the Liberation House.

It had been a really long night, getting woken up at three AM with pounding on our door again. Someone else from church coming off drugs needing support. It was a frequent thing this past year. We were hundreds of people now at Faith Center and the Scripture where it talks about "with the strength of the oxen comes the mess" made so much more sense to me now... There were some beautiful people coming through our doors that were falling in love with Jesus and some were instantly delivered of their afflictions and addictions but others were wrestling, and sometimes they needed help at three in the morning.

The bicycle ride had woken me up though. I inhaled the fresh air and then looked up at the gray house with its white trim and wooden sign hanging from the porch beam that read: Liberation House.

"Hi Roy!" I was greeted by Dan Purkey, the devoted man leading this place. I pushed my bike up to the porch and leaned it against the railing. Not unlike Shiloh where I'd first seen hippies getting saved, this house was a place for men to grow in spiritual and life disciplines. They came as a group to Faith Center every service we had! The new building was filling up just like the old one was. We'd been meeting in the gymnasium and Dan would bring the most interesting people we'd seen so far through the doors.

"Hey Dan, I thought I'd stop by and see this place, with all the characters you keep bringing to church and what you've got going on here." I smiled at him with a teasing grin. I was genuinely curious. Dan smiled and led me into the house.

"Yes come in, let me show you around," he replied.

As he showed me the set up of the house and explained the three month system he'd set up and things he looked for in character development that they worked on, through disciplines and routines, my thoughts drifted to the guy he'd brought to my office a few months ago that was clearly demonized.

Dan hadn't been very confident at that time in how to help this tormented man. We saw a lot of mental illness come through our pastor and elder doors. It could be serious life threatening situations and then there were the times we just needed to do deliverance. In this particular circumstance the man Dan had brought over had quickly started manifesting something but then instantly relaxed when I'd told the spirit to be gone and it couldn't stay, in Jesus name. I could tell it made Dan uncomfortable, and he'd brought 2-3 more people over for deliverance ministry before I realized we should be teaching people to do this themselves. After discussing with Noel Campbell and other leaders, we agreed we needed to switch discipleship tactics to equipping others to do these things and hear from the Lord for themselves vs relying on the pastors and elders for help all the time.

"We let people stay three nights for free with no commitment but they have to either wander the sidewalks or join us when going to church. We don't leave them alone in the house," Dan was explaining as we circled back to the front porch bringing me out of my recollections. He really did have a good system going on here in this house. Any doubts or questions I'd had were put to rest as I hopped back on my bike.

"If you need anything Dan, just let me know. Give me a call." I put my hand on his shoulder reassuringly. He nodded and I started to wheel my bike out to the street. I gave him a little wave and headed home. We were headed out later today for a skiing trip to Utah. I was finally getting the hang of the sport although my love for speed inevitably had me crashing and burning each day on those slopes. Paul Berg was teaching me and it was amazing. The air you could get was exhilarating even if it did inevitably tend to end in my colliding into something. It was worth it and I was excited for the time away with friends. No interrupted nights. No theological questions. No crisis to fix.

Brenda on the piano had worked out beautifully. Although I could tell it still wasn't her favorite thing to do, she had figured it out. She and her husband Paul had become such good friends of ours. Paul owned a ski shop so during the off season he'd arrange skiing trips for us all, I wasn't really into it but the others would do puzzles in the evenings after we'd hit the slopes and their patience amazed me. These breaks were so necessary. I was so looking forward to it.

These days my schedule was packed but I had submitted it to the elders in the church. Letting them choose which guest speaking opportunities that kept being sent my way by various other churches and ministries I should take. The elders were very supportive however of Kay and me taking time away, they knew we needed it. I could almost smell the snow and hear the rush of the skis over it despite the warming spring sun beating down on me as I pedaled home. It was going to be great.

<u>Roy's story continues in Chapter 21</u>

Roy preaching in the park

Faith Center gathering in the park.

Roy preaching in the sanctuasium.

Chapter 12

Flutes & Faith

Erik's Story

1973 - Central Park - New York City

A yellow taxi honked its way past the park entrance as a crowd of tourists and New Yorkers watched me continue my pantomime. I silently moved with humorous moves acting out my street skit. A few kids stopped to join my audience. They were probably about ten years old. So different from when I was roaming these streets when I was their age. Back then, bopping had been the in-thing, which was walking like a tough gorilla. I'd combed my ten year old hair back with grease, snapping my fingers, and my friends and I pretended we were in a gang. Ten had been a fun age until that fateful drive through this park. We'd thought we were going to an event but really they'd taken us to the airport and my mom moved us without warning to Argentina for three years to escape Dad.

Coming back to my childhood friends three years later had been a culture shock. They had all changed. Greasy hair wasn't the in thing anymore. It had changed to marajuana, the needle, anti war protests, and dropping out of school. I'd quickly discovered how dangerous that drug scene was. I'd pulled away from my hardcore friends after watching my little brother's life get destroyed with them. And the few Students for a Democratic Society (SDS) meetings I'd gone to with college kids and organized high school leftists hadn't spoken my language. That political scene of anger and intended violence only seemed to lead to more violence. It had brought back memories of my volatile father when he was a prisoner to the bottle and I'd stopped going. It freaked me out. So I'd been traveling and doing street theater since leaving home at seventeen a few years ago.

A young woman in my audience plopped a whole dollar bill in my bucket. I gave her my clownish happy smile and blew her a kiss to the delight of the children in my audience. I returned to my mime as she walked away to find my audience was staring off to my right distracted with something. I did a robot turn staying in character to investigate my competition.

Some in the audience were pointing now to a gray suited man walking my way. I did an exaggerated squint with my hand over my eyes in his direction and recognition and shock filled me. I controlled the emotion and searched for the appropriate dramatic mime gesture as he came to a stop in front of me. It was Ed Sullivan. The man who had made the Beatles famous in the USA. In the flesh. I gave a dramatic bow and pretended a fainting spell. Which wasn't as much acting as it was a real indication of my own internal state that I had this influential man's attention!

"What's your name?" He laughed at my antics.

Should I break character and answer? If I didn't I'd never get a chance like this again in my life. I pulled my voice out of an invisible cup and said, "It's Erik Sampson, Mr. Sullivan."

"I enjoyed your schtick. I would like to write you up in my column in the papers." He smiled.

Maybe choosing the street theater life in New York City was finally going to pay off.

1974 - Big Island, Hawaii (One Year Later)

The giant tree above me stood firm in the tropical breeze. I enjoyed the isolation of this little spot at the end of the road. Nothing had come out of that meeting with Ed Sullivan a year ago. I'd continued my flute making and sold them to fund my travels. I'd changed from being a radical of my high school years to a spiritual hippie. I loved a good spiritual conversation.

A young man and woman in their Sunday best were coming out of a church service in the distance. They were walking in my direction. Were they coming over to me? I looked around my tree for any other source of their odd focus. I was at the literal dead end of this street! They were still coming towards me. The young man handed the woman his Bible and made eye contact.

Great. Were these going to be the kind of bulldog Christians who just want to make me feel bad and beat me up with their aggressive words or would they instead be like the nice Christian guy at the papaya farm, a cool friend of Jesus. I prepared myself. I was ready.

A Few Days Later

Relief washed over me as I pushed my way through the jungle underbrush and found the abandoned Hippie commune I'd been told about. Among the vines, giant grass and mold that had overtaken the place was a Bible. What were the odds? I brought it back to the lean-to I was living in, underneath an avocado tree about a mile away on the mountain. A few days earlier a Christian guy on the road that I was walking on wanted me to promise to read the Bible. And now I'd found one.

There wasn't anything else to do up here. I flipped through the book of John for a bit and then pulled a magazine out of my bag. This girl at the health food store had given it to me. I flipped it open to a story about Ron Depriest. He'd been a really mean biker who came to Christ. I didn't seem to be able to escape from these Jesus Freaks! The biker's story talked about how God had been greater than this guy's anger, hate and violence. I flipped to the next page. His powerful story was stirring something in me. Was I a sinner like he had been? What does sin even mean?

The tragedy of my girlfriend in Guatemala telling me she was pregnant and me telling her to go get an abortion came back to my memory. I had really blown it during my life. The guilt slammed me again. Is this what sin was? These things we intuitively knew were wrong? The consequences of my lifestyle choices? Were all these things separating me from God?

I fell back in defeat onto my bed. "Ok Jesus. I can see that I am a sinner. Separated from You and that's why I need You. Would you please take away my sins and forgive me and come into my heart." I closed my eyes, holding back tears. A moment went by and suddenly something soothing warmed my feet and continued up my ankles. What on earth! The warmth spread up my legs to my torso and enveloped my whole being. A peace I couldn't explain settled over my mind and heart. Such a deep peace....

I woke up. It was morning! Something was different. I could feel it. I didn't know what was happening to me. But I bet that papaya farmer would.

I went down the mountain and found the farmer. "Hi", is all I could say and I just stared at him.

A knowing look crossed his face, "Erik, have you come to trust Jesus as your savior?"

I nodded yes.

Tears almost came from his eyes and he wrapped his arms around me. "Brother!"

He held me out at arms length with a joy I'd never seen on him before. "You need to pull away from everyone and dive into the Bible. Ask the Lord to open your eyes to His word, His truth, and His love."

1975 - New York (One Year Later)

I stepped off the greyhound bus in Woodstock, New York. I was trying to put together a new traveling theater troupe that had a similar heart for Jesus. My new friend Raysun, who happened to be living in the same bamboo hut I had stayed in months before, was coming up from Florida to help me. She was enjoying the Gospel of John that I'd given her when I'd tried to escape the cold New York winter. While I waited for Raysun to arrive, I'd headed up to Woodstock.

"Hey, man, are you coming tonight?" A burly bearded guy asked from across the street.

"Coming where?"

"You know, to the Community Center? Some of the Rainbow Farm freaks got saved and they're going to talk tonight."

"Oh, how about that. Ok sure." I followed him down a few blocks to where the meeting would be held. Next door was a meditation place that was announcing a gathering that night too. If the Christian gathering did not pan out, I would go check that out.

It took a little while at the Community Center but the Christians began to arrive. The men were wearing suits and I had a feeling this was not going to be my cup of tea. This was not the kind of Christian I wanted to be. I didn't want to be a suit wearing Christian! I looked around for the exit and found a door towards the back. I wasn't going to be this kind of Jesus's disciple. Not my thing at all. I just wanted to be me.

I stood up and left the room, walked to the meditation place and opened a side door. A hot wall of incense smoke hit me. I could hardly breathe. A huge crowd filled the big dark hazy meditation room. The realization hit me, these were all lost souls in there that were stuck. I closed the door and returned to the Christian meeting.

Different people were talking now and they looked more like me. I sat down on a wooden chair in the back. They shared similar salvation experiences like I'd had!

Finally the suited preacher said, "Who would like to get filled by the Holy Spirit?"

Nobody raised their hands. What did that even mean filled with the spirit? I leaned back in my chair and glanced over the crowd to see if anyone was raising their hand behind me when suddenly pain shot through my rear as part of the chair pinched me and I shot up to my feet. When I stood up everyone looked at me.

"Great! Let's gather around this young man and pray for him."

I stared at the preacher in shock. What was happening? I wasn't about to say the chair pinched me! Well who doesn't want the Spirit of God? I relaxed. I'll just go with the flow.

The Christians laid their hands on me and I felt that familiar warm sensation settle on me. This was the real deal. This was that same thing I'd experienced in my lean-to under the avocado tree in Hawaii but this time it was much more intense! Like a holy fire exploding inside of me. I had to bring Raysun to meet these people!

Six Months Later - Faith Center - Eugene, Oregon

I'd just watched Raysun eat a hot dog at lunch for the first time in our short relationship. I'd thought she was a true vegetarian. "I prayed over it," she'd told my judgmental facial expressions. I wasn't sold on this temporary place we were staying at on our traveling road trip. It was a Christian discipleship house and I was glad of the company but Raysun was changing fast and I didn't know if I wanted her to.

Now we were here at a gym, a sign over the door read, "Jesus Christ the same yesterday today and forever." The place was packed! My jaw dropped as I followed our new Lib House friends to a section of the place. There were Hippie looking people like me. There were straight suit people too. All mingling together. I couldn't believe the hundreds of people in this place! This was just one church in one city in one country in the whole world. Could there really be this many people out there that loved Jesus this much? That were changing their lives and gathering in communities like this? Was God really moving on this many people's hearts as He had mine?

We came to Eugene to sell flutes at the fair that we never found. We had success at the Saturday Market yesterday and Raysun had told me she was going to stay here in Eugene. I didn't want to leave without her so we'd committed to the house's three month mentorship and character building program. What was wild was that at that market a girl had come up and shared with us her testimony and how after she'd gotten saved she'd gone to this hippie commune on Big Island and left a Bible there. It was the same book I'd then picked up not a few days later at my own trip to that commune! What were the odds of a connection like that! I'd told her the book had borne fruit and how I had gotten saved and been taking a slow growth path to understanding the faith but it had led us here.

Raysun had come to New York and gotten saved at that church of those believers who had gone up to Woodstock. We'd both gotten baptized there too. I felt so close to that woman. We'd exchanged tender letters for a few months until I got a van and then I'd gone and picked her up to begin a theater tour with a spiritual message, selling flutes along the way to pay our way. She was gorgeous but we'd both been burned by the free love Hippie culture. We'd agreed early on we were going to keep our distance. We were sure the Lib House was the right place at the perfect time for us and we melted into this community that loved Jesus. This place and these people were going to be good for us.

A Month Later - Dan Purkey's Truck - Lib House - Eugene, Oregon

Everything was suddenly black. I couldn't move, I couldn't talk. I'd gotten to the point in my testimony where I was talking about an astral projection conference

I attended and Dan was sitting with me in his truck having asked me to share my story with him. Suddenly darkness gripped my soul. This wasn't like anything I'd experienced before.

"Erik? Are you ok?" Dan asked.

I was still paralyzed unable to speak. What was happening to me?

Dan put his hand on my shoulder "I bind you devil, in Jesus name. Let him go! He was bought by the blood of Jesus Christ the Son of God and belongs to God."

The blackness lifted. My breath returned to its natural rhythm and peace filled the void the fear had left.

"Ya, I'm ok now. Thank you! That was totally weird!"

"You know brother, you need deliverance from this stuff. And part of your healing process is to not even talk about these things because you begin to glorify them. You are a new creature now."

I nodded. Dan was great at discipling the people in Lib House. I realized I was growing slowly and Raysun quickly. I'd really disliked that she was wearing colored clothing. Before she only wore white. I didn't like that she took back her real name, Linda. And that she was eating meat. How powerful was what was going on at the Lib House that she was becoming a new person. She was wearing bras and growing up in her faith without me. But I couldn't deny the changes I was noticing in my own life as much as hers. This place had been just what we needed to build the foundation of our faith. I was thankful for our time here, but it was coming to a close.

A Month Later

I had been driving for hours and not gotten sleepy! Typically I only made it 1-2 hours before Linda needed to take over. The Lib house people had prayed for us as we left a day ago to head home to Florida. I must've gotten free of something or healed of something. I drove for nine hours straight! Driving was a delight now but we were coming up on a critical point in our route. If we took the northern route back east, the weather was bad, the roads were snowy. We didn't have snow chains. I pulled over and stopped. We needed to pray.

"What's going on?" One of the two hitchhikers we'd picked up a few hours ago asked as he exchanged a strange look with his friend.

"I'm going to get out and pray."

"Ok. Good plan." Linda agreed.

"I need God to show me if I should take the cold northern route or the southern route which is a thousand miles out of the way. Or perhaps stop in Berkeley at an old commune to pick up a Giant puppet." I explained as best I could and hopped out of the van. Linda joined me.

I kneeled down to the ground and closed my eyes and prayed. God, which way should we go?

Silence.

I opened my eyes. Linda sat nearby drawing in the sand with a stick as she silently prayed. I closed my eyes again. Which way should we go....

A picture of an E appeared in my mind. The bottom part of the letter was pulsing.

The southernmost part of the letter!

The south route!

I opened my eyes again to see Linda finishing the bottom part of a letter E in the dirt.

"That was exactly what I saw Linda!"

"What do you mean?" She looked at me confused.

"Nevermind. It's just the Lord's confirmation. We are going to take the southern route. Not the northern route and we are not going to Berkeley, we're going East by the southern route."

This new faith in God was so incredible. He really did answer our prayers. He really did direct our ways! He was really changing us. I hugged Linda and testified, drunk with joy, to those in the car that God guides and provides. No more darkness clouded our days. We'd been set free and we were heading home with a new foundation that couldn't be shaken.

> *He has shown you, O man, what is*
> *good; And what does the Lord require*
> *of you But to do justly, To love mercy,*
> *And to walk humbly with your God?*
> **Micah 6:8 NKJV**

Erik and Linda were true to their commitment and saved themselves for their marriage on Oct 9th, 1976. On their honeymoon in Guatemala they began sharing the gospel through simple skits and sparked the beginnings of their traveling theatrical ministry around the globe. They currently live on an acre of bamboo in Florida making flutes and working with a team that helps manage 105 feeding centers and 300 special needs kids in Nicaragua. Erik and Linda have been able to minister in Israel, the Caribbean and all throughout the Americas from Argentina to Canada. He and Linda went on to have five children and now have nine grandchildren. In 2010 he published a book called Bumping into God that contains the full testimony of his life.[1] You can get a copy at his website Eriktheflutemaker.com. You can also read more about their ministry at flutemakerministries.org

You can read Linda's story in the following chapter.
You can read Dan Purkey's story in Becoming Jesus People Volume 1.

---

1. Erik Sampson, "Bumping Into God:The Story of Eric the Flutemaker," (Florida: Self Published,2011)

Erik making flutes

Erik and Linda

Chapter 13

I'm Staying!

Linda's Story

**February 1975 - Maya House (House of Illusion Commune)
- Coconut Grove, Florida**

The turquoise beads were running low. I needed five more to complete the necklace. I lifted up my bed mat, searching for any dropped stragglers. Aha! Some had rolled over to the book of John that my new friend Erik had left me a few months ago. It was interesting, like Erik. He gave off the typical spiritual guru vibe but he talked about Jesus instead. Most of the guru followers in this commune were all consumed with themselves. Seems like the quest for enlightenment made us all feel so important and powerful and yet we were so confused and conflicted with one another. I found myself very tired of the hippie hypocrisy that I'd been living with for a few years while creating jewelry to make ends meet.

There was more than one way to connect to the divine, wasn't there? Yoga, meditation, Buddhism, Hinduism, and Christianity were all just different avenues to God as far as I was concerned. I'd grown up Episcopalian but I couldn't get over the idea there had to be more ways to God. Christianity felt so narrow and yet I was willing to take another look at it. Because of Erik.

"Raysun! That dude Erik is back again looking for you!", a girl from the Maya House called through the thin wall of my hut.

He was here! I shoved my jewelry making tools into the storage box. I looked out the hut to see Erik. He had the warmest smile. I might be falling for him, but I really didn't need a new relationship right now.

"Hey Raysun!" He embraced me.

"Erik I'm so glad you're back!"

"Ya I am trying to put together a traveling theater troupe but hoping to stick with people that are interested in Jesus. I thought of you! Do you want to come up to New York and help me pick out a van and then go on the road together?"

It sounded like an adventure. "Yes!" I wanted to know more about this guy and how he understood Jesus. I was creative. I could do theater. "Yes I would love that!"

A Month Later - Pentecostal Church - New York City

Erik had insisted I come check out these new Christian friend's he'd met. The building was musky and cold and I couldn't help comparing how it felt to the warmth of the Florida sun I'd grown up in. But the people were kind, vibrant even, and very friendly. I could see the appeal he was talking about. There was life here. Erik sat next to me in the pew still wearing his tunic with a large head of buddha on the back. He didn't look like the other Christians here. We were definitely the most hippie looking in the place. The preacher was giving a message that I think was targeted at Erik with his long hair and flowing looking garb. But he seemed genuine in his passion for what he was preaching.

"If you want to give your life to Jesus, I invite you to come forward." He finished his message. Something was pulling on my heart. I wanted to know. I closed my eyes. *God, if Jesus really is the ONLY way to you I ask you to show me.*

Blue light surrounded me. The sounds disappeared and the seat beneath me vanished. Where was I? What was this? I wasn't on any drugs, this was not a drug trip! Was this God answering my silent prayer? This blue hue felt peaceful. Calming. I could stay here forever. What would happen if I opened my eyes? Would this vision end?

I risked it. I opened my eyes a sliver.

"Looks like our sister is ready to receive Jesus! Will you all pray with me for her?" I heard the preacher say and discovered myself at the altar! How had I gotten here?! I repeated the prayer the pastor led me through.

"Let's go downstairs and get you two baptized." I saw Erik next to me now beaming. The pastor must have meant him too. I followed them all in a daze down a few flights of stairs into a room with a baptismal tank, and a group of very excited Christians! The women led me to a private place to change into a white robe so my clothes would stay dry. I re-entered the room with the tank and they submerged me. The baptizer, with loud joyous authority, made a declaration and submerged me, and as I came up I felt cleaner than I ever knew was possible. Something changed! I stepped out dripping onto a mat and a woman handed me a towel. Then it was Erik's turn. I remember thinking, 'I wish I never had to take off this robe that I just got baptized in. This is the most incredible feeling I've ever had.' Everyone was singing praises at our new birth and I wanted to join them. I felt like a brand new person in a matter of moments! I didn't know how much heavy weight and darkness I'd been carrying until it was gone. I just wanted to stay living in this moment. I didn't want this feeling to ever leave me.

This must be Jesus.

This must be God.

Six Months Later - Maya House - Coconut Grove, Florida

Erik's latest letter stuck out from my Bible on the little table in my hut. It used to have books from many different gurus occupying its space. I removed them all and placed my Bible in the center. Erik was finally arriving today, after half a year of correspondence since our baptisms in New York City. He'd gotten everything set to travel and share Jesus with people through puppet shows! My feelings for him were growing.

I packed up the last few things in my hut. This place had been my home for over a year now. It was going to be interesting to be on the road doing street theater and gently bringing the message of Jesus. Erik was thinking we could also pass by LA to collect clothes to give to the poor in Mexico.

I was truly ready for a change. Ever since I'd come back to the commune it hadn't felt the same. Many times in the middle of the night I would hear screaming and sense darkness all around me, bringing with it paralyzing fear. This had never happened before I went to New York. Something had changed. It was freaky. Whenever it happened I'd find peace in the full moon lit nights reading Psalm 23 or reciting the Lord's Prayer that I still recalled from my childhood. It got me through those terrifying nights and through the days where I felt stuck in a maze. When I asked the other people living in the commune about the night noises no one knew what I was talking about. It was all so very strange.

I found two other people in the commune who had a love for Jesus. We had some fascinating conversations around the dinner table about the Book of Revelation. One guy had come out of the cult of Moses David and the other was a backslidden Jehovah's Witness, a father to one of the other hippies also living there. We couldn't stop talking about Jesus. I was thankful for them in the midst of all the other seekers touting various ways to commune with the divine.

So now everything was packed. I picked up my Bible and held it close to my heart. I was ready for a new adventure.

October 1975 - Mount Shasta, California

"Hey, good evening. I smelled something very nice coming from here. Wow, are those flutes you're making?" A nearby camper asked, walking over to where Erik sat by a fire burning about a dozen flutes. I turned over the potatoes I was roasting on the campfire. My legs still ached from the long climb up this mountain a few days ago. Someone had told us it was free to live up here so we set up camp. We would go to town to buy food and supplies, selling flutes that Erik made to pay for our needs.

"Yes it is, these are minor flutes from bamboo we just harvested in Florida," Erik responded.

"You know, there's this incredible art fair about to happen in Eugene, Oregon where folks come from all over and trade with one another and sell their stuff. You should really consider going to it."

"Really?" I asked for both of us.

"Really! I bet you would do really well selling your flutes there."

We hadn't had a show for about a month and the money was starting to run out.

"How far is Eugene from here?" Erik asked the man as he started to walk away.

"Oh not too bad, probably about a four hour drive."

"Thanks man."

"Yup, no problem."

Erik looked at me. We had the same thought. We finished our dinner and started packing.

"I think this could be God providing for us Raysun," Erik said as he rolled up his tools and put them in the van. I nodded and headed over to the tent we shared to help him collapse it.

The moon was a big help as we packed up our things and hopped in the van. We got onto Interstate 5 and traveled all night through the mountain fog.

Daylight sprung, the fog eased, and we could see we were on top of a mountain. Finally we found our way to Eugene. We parked and walked around asking people about the famous craft fair but no one knew what we were talking about. No one! Where would we go now? What were we going to do? We jumped into the van and began to drive.

Erik pulled over for a fellow asking for a ride.

"Thanks guys. Where are you heading?"

"Actually we don't know, we are looking for a big fair where craftsmen come from all over and trade with each other and sell. We are flutemakers and do street theater too. Do you know where this is?" Erik asked frustratedly.

"No man, but if you need a place to stay, there is a cool place called The Liberation House. You can stay there up to three days. Then if you want to connect and join with them you help out and move in. It's down this road and on my way, so I will show you where it is."

I looked at Erik. Was God providing for us a place to stay, so we could recoup at this moment of our journey? We parked under one of the giant trees on Mill street and walked into the huge house. A sign hung off the porch with the name Jesus on it! It was a community of Jesus followers!

"How can we help you?" This tall brown haired man opened the door.

"We need a place to stay for the night. Someone mentioned you take people in? We're Christians too!" I answered.

"That's awesome! Yes we have room for you but the men's guest space is full."

"It's ok I can sleep in our van," Erik offered.

"I was about to head out on a walk. Why don't you come with me and tell me your testimony. I'm Riley, one of the house elders." He offered his hand to Erik.

"Definitely!" Erik took his hand. Riley was in for a big story. Some of the ladies in the house welcomed me in. How exciting this new adventure was, filled with such love and joy.

1975 - Eugene Saturday Market

Another person picked up my 'Make a joyful noise unto the Lord' inscribed flute and then dropped it in protest and continued to another booth. I was in charge of sanding and had been engraving little verses on the bamboo barrels.

"You're going to quench sales with those things Raysun!" Erik grumbled as he adjusted some of his flutes in our makeshift booth he'd constructed with bamboo. We'd sold a few flutes already and the entrance fee to this market was minimal. It wasn't anything like an art fair but it was working.

"I'm leaving, Raysun." My heart sank. He was leaving Eugene? He didn't want to stay at the Christian home? The Lib House had turned out to be so amazing! Why would he want to leave? It was a true Christian community. Everyone was learning, growing and encouraging one another daily. I'd had the deepest conversations there than ever in my life! The shepherdess Stephie and the other woman Lindsay had been so welcoming and helpful to me. Even my conversations with Riley were changing the way I understood my faith. I was starting to wonder if I should go back to my real name: Linda. Raysun had been what I'd adopted in my life as a hippie and I wasn't sure I wanted to be that way anymore.

I held back tears at the thought of Erik leaving, and me staying. They'd told us there was room if we wanted to commit to the three month program of daily quiet times, work crew, church attendance, Scripture memorization, etc. I thought Erik was the one. That we would be together for the rest of our lives. He'd been such a gentleman and we'd agreed early on to keep our relationship sexually pure. We both were done with all that the hippie kingdom offered and we'd been true to our word. But I loved him. If I stayed, I would lose him.

But I loved Jesus more. He was transforming my life in a way I hadn't thought possible. He'd led us to this house and these people that were challenging me and answering all my questions with grace and joy. Jesus was my priority, He was the most important one in my entire life right now.

Tearing up I answered him with a ton of surrender, "Well Erik. I'm staying." I said it before I could change my mind. I was going to let him go.

His eyes suddenly got wide and teary as it dawned on him what I thought he was saying. After an eternal moment of silence he tenderly and sheepishly blurted out, "I didn't mean I was leaving the Lib House or you, just the booth to clear my mind".

I fought against a smile. We both held each other in a strong embrace. I had put God first, the business issues would take care of themselves. Like maybe having a few Scripture flutes and many plain flutes.

1975 Liberation House

Lindsay and I finished getting ready for church in the steamy bathroom that one of the other girls had just finished showering in. It was a bit squished on Sunday mornings. I loved Lindsay's brown jean skirt. I could probably sew something like it. She smiled at me in the mirror as she finished brushing her hair.

"We are leaving in five minutes ladies!" The house shepherdess Stephie called up the stairs. I adjusted my new bra under my sweater. I had asked Lindsay and Stephie to help me buy one a month ago. Sure it was definitely less comfortable than the freedom I had without it but I didn't really care anymore about that. I cared more about dressing appropriately. I loved these people that I was getting to know and I wanted to be a blessing to them. I'd sent a letter to my sister in Florida asking her to send me some normal clothes as I was getting rid of my whole hippie wardrobe. I was changing inside and out.

I made my way down the narrow staircase and into the car that took us to church. God was using this community to leave His footprints on my heart. Even contributing through chores for the good of the house was important to me. I remembered Erik and I putting too much peanut butter on all the sandwiches one day and Phil making us redo them before Dan found out. They were on a budget and apparently we had used up a few days worth of peanut butter! It had been a pain but we did it. We participated in everything they asked of us and we both began to grow in wonderful ways.

The car parked in a spot near the church entrance. We always came early because the place was always packed. I followed my Lib House brothers and sisters into the gym and we sat in our regular section as a group. The rest of the gym filled up in the next few minutes as we anticipated the start of the service. During worship, Erik and I sang our hearts out. Roy got up to speak.

"There are hundreds of us in this room but we can never know hundreds of people well. Who can tell me who were Jesus's closest disciples?" He asked from the pulpit.

One of the lib house brothers raised his hands.

"Yes." Roy pointed at him.

"Peter, James, and John!" .

"Yes! I know I can always count on you Lib Housers to have the answer." Roy laughed and the congregation followed suit, filling the hollow arched ceiling with echoes. The carpet only did so much to dampen the acoustics. But the reverberation did make for an amazing acapella worship time. Roy continued with his sermon and I couldn't believe how fortunate I was to be here right now. To be surrounded by a family of other believers growing and seeking the Lord together.

A Month Later

I polished the stairwell rails as best as I could. I was doing all of my chores the night before we left because it was so important to me. Riley saw me and yelled from the bottom of the stairs, "Linda, you're leaving tomorrow. You don't have to do that."

"This place has given me so much, it's a tiny way I can give back." I responded.

After living here for two wonderful months, Erik and I were heading back to Florida to be with our family for Christmas. We'd both been transformed in our short time here. I loved this place. It was going to be hard to leave.

I turned back to the rails. I was going to get them to sparkle. Just like I felt on the inside. Like a gem. Jesus had found me and now I knew my true identity, I was a precious, blood-bought daughter of the King. This house and all I learned here, was so precious to me. I wanted to leave it well.

He that dwelleth in the secret place of
the most High shall abide under the
shadow of the Almighty. I will say of
the LORD, He is my refuge and my
fortress: my God; in him will I trust.
Psalms 91: 1-2 KJV

Linda's time at Lib House was so memorable and so defining for the rest of her walk with Christ. She and Erik got married in 1976. For their honeymoon they went to Guatemala and started doing Christian theater there, birthing a creative drama ministry. They traveled, sharing the gospel through powerful yet simple theatrical skits for many years. They also took many people into their home in the style of what they learned at Liberation House. They are currently supporting a ministry in Nicaragua that helps special needs children and sends containers of food to help many who struggle with food insecurity in Nicaragua and Guatemala. They live on a bamboo plantation in Florida and have five kids and nine grandkids. You can read more about their ministry at and flute making business at eriktheflutemake r.com.

You can read Dan, Riley, Lindsay, and Stephie's stories in Becoming Jesus People Volume 1.[1]

Linda & Erik's Wedding

New parents on the road for Jesus.

---

1. Carissa Gobble and Riley Taylor, "Becoming Jesus People:True Stories of How Love Broke Through In The Jesus People Movement," (GPC Publishing, 2023), 9-12 & 149-154, 35-44, 89-96.

Chapter 14

Road Trip Gone Wild!

Nancy's Story

August 1975 - Cody, Wyoming

"Nancy, you've got a call!" Mrs. Read hollered from the Deer Creek Ranch cookhouse. I came out from the kitchen and took the receiver from her.

"Hello?"

"Hey Nancy, it's Sue."

"Oh hey Sue! I can't wait for our west coast road trip in a few weeks!"

"Ya....that's why I'm calling. I'm back in Michigan."

"What?"

"Ya my aunt just died. I'm sorry. I'm not going to be able to make our trip. I'm so disappointed but I have to be here. I already signed up for classes next term."

Speechless, my heart sank. As housemates at Michigan State, we were both working on ranches out west for the summer and had big dreams to backpack and travel the west coast once we were done. We'd made a master plan for this road trip! Organized all the details. Nothing left to chance. Figured out all the stops. Would be purchasing the Greyhound America unlimited pass for two months. Knew which friends we wanted to visit. The sights we wanted to see. We'd never been to the west coast before and now here she was bailing on me last minute!

"Nancy? You still there?"

"Ugh. Ya this really is a bummer."

"I know. I know! I'm so sorry. Do you think you'll still go?"

Still go?

All alone?

I guess I could. I'd come out here to Wyoming last summer in an attempt to escape the mass of 40,000 college age party animals, of which I was one, and hopefully "find myself". Mrs. Read had hired me over only a letter correspondence and it had turned out great. The wilderness was exactly what I had needed and I'd come back here this summer planning to take the whole next term off school and road trip with Sue. I don't think I could still register for classes that started up in a few weeks. Maybe I should still go. I was already halfway out here in Cody, Wyoming after all.

"Maybe I will."

"Good for you! You should totally do it and then come back in a few months and tell me all about it!"

"Ok. Sue."

"Have the best time Nancy!"

"I'll try."

We exchanged pleasant goodbyes and I hung up.

NOW what was I going to do??

A solo trip was definitely not my plan! Oh sure, I'd traveled alone before, but for 2 months? And on a bus full of strangers?! Lugging my backpack with all my earthly possessions and tent while truckin' around in hiking boots? But this was the 70's! Everyone was traveling this way and hitchhiking was another mode of transportation, of which I was also familiar. But going alone meant I had to call my parents...I picked up the receiver again and twisted the dial in circles for each number. This would be no easy conversation....

"Hello?"

"Hello, Mother"

"Oh, Nancy dear....just a minute while I call your father to pick up the other line....Dick! It's Nancy on the phone!"

"Well, well...if it's not our ranch hand daughter! Been ridin' any horses lately? Seen any more bears?" It was always good to hear my daddy's jovial voice.

"Not lately. I've been busy getting packed and organized for the big bus adventure. Some of my belongings won't fit in my backpack or not needed so I'll be sending home a package next week. But about the trip...well...Sue won't be going now."

"What's that? Sue won't be going? Does that mean you will be coming home?" My anxious mother was beginning to freak out at the thought of what I would say next.

"No, Mother, I am not coming home. I am going forward with the trip...alone...and I will be careful. Besides, I have a very detailed plan which I expect to follow to the letter. I just have to do this."

"Oh Nancy dear, plans can change. You don't have to prove anything".

I could hear the emotion in her voice.

"Well, I'm afraid my mind is made up. And I promise to call collect from a pay phone every Sunday so you can hear my voice and know I am alive!" I supposed that would be reassuring...for them and for me. I was in charge of my own life as much as I loved my parents and knew they cared. I was determined to take this trip...and that was that!

October 1975 - On a Greyhound Bus
- The Washington/Oregon Border

"Ya get petrified if you don't move around," the kindly old woman who had been my seatmate on this leg of my trip from Bellingham to Eugene said as she sat back down. I guess her words held more than physical meaning. We had to keep moving in some way shape or form to further our self growth. Stagnation was death. I should write that down.

I reached down to pull my journal out of the large backpack I was traveling with. The tent attachment I'd let the driver put in the undercarriage storage compartments. It would be safe there. Unlike my new expensive down jacket that had gotten stolen within the first few days of my trip. That misfortune had totally thrown off my plan, yet it led me to new friends who'd taken pity on my cold jacketless self, causing a slight detour to Vancouver, Canada with them.

I flipped open my journal and caught my first entry from a week ago.

> *Up until now, for the past week, I have discovered an order to my life which has gone unnoticed up to this point. Why? What did I do before that time that disguised this obvious pattern? Living life, unaware of its basis, "caught up" in nothingness, such as routine, is like fighting nature. Spontaneity. It is life. It is now MY life.*

Something was happening on this trip I couldn't explain. There was no way I could have imagined or planned for the interesting people I had already met. Like the cool girl, Marian, who had hitchhiked with a guy all the way from New York, or the especially large, talkative man who fell asleep on my shoulder on the bus at three AM! And then there were the unplanned destinations like Seattle, Vancouver and Victoria. Or the massive ten dollars a night I paid at a swanky hotel! I was somewhat awed by the new friends and adventures transpiring outside my carefully laid plans. It was like someone behind the scenes was orchestrating a movie script and I was the heroine. I felt an overwhelming need to document its uniqueness. This thing I was discovering about myself. My love of control and order and the wonder that was to be found in the unexpected surprised me. How had I not known this about myself before? I'd tried to call Sam, my old boyfriend from high school, to wish him happy birthday all the way over in Hawaii a few days ago but hadn't gotten through.

I finished up my next entry as the driver gave us a five minute warning to the next rest stop.

So this morning I left Bellingham (early) taking with me very fond memories of wonderful people and beautiful places. I'm coming to discover that it is the people you meet that make all the difference. Growth and learning come from those valuable interactions, those precious exchanges and sharing of thoughts with another human being. From each person you gain another piece of the answer as to who you really are. I'm on my way to Eugene--get ready for me 'Genie, baby!

That Evening - Mill St - Eugene, Oregon

Dusk was fast diminishing into night as I scanned the house numbers for 1262. I'd found Mill Street easy enough after calling the YWCA to ask if they'd had any accommodations for the night. I'd been disappointed. They'd given me two numbers of other houses in the city to try and Liberation House had sounded like the most hip and promising of the two. I'd called that one and a guy answered and gave me the address and directions. There were a lot of voices in the background like a party. Good sign! It should be coming up here soon. Maybe that one - five or six houses down with the bright yellow hippie van!

I was excited. I wonder what far-out people I'll meet in this city! I was one house away now and I was right! It was 1262! Yes! A Liberation House sign hung from the awning but there was another sign.

Jesus is Lord.

I stopped in my tracks. WHAT?! Oh great. It was a Jesus freak commune! I'd had enough of those people in my life. Sure, I'd grown up in church and my grandparents had made faith look appealing for a while but then they were gone and I had been happy to escape the confines of my parents' house for the parties and freedom of college. But then my super fun roommate Shirley, had become a Christian and turned out to be the dorkiest friend, going to church and all. Then there'd been that other roommate, Kris, a year ago, that would read her Bible every single morning. At least she hadn't preached at me. But still, these were not my kind of people. It was going to be a rough night. Maybe I'll find a different place tomorrow. I mounted the five steps to the landing and knocked on the door.

They'd told me on the phone I could stay for three nights but I didn't think I was going to need them. A young man opened the door and welcomed me in. He must've been the guy on the phone. It was like he'd expected me. I walked into the front room and realized there was some sort of gathering happening. The space was filled to the brim with people smiling....having a Bible study!

"Hi!" There was a chorus of greetings.

"Hi, I'm Nancy."

"Welcome Nancy!"

How had I ended up here?

"Can I take your backpack?" A young woman with short cropped brown hair and the sweetest eyes offered. "My name's Lindsay. I'll go put it up in our women's guest room."

"Um... sure." I sloughed it off my shoulders and gave it to her... suddenly disarmed by the approval and love that seemed to radiate from her and the others in the room. Any fear of losing more of my belongings had vanished. What was this place?

"Come join us, Nancy."

I felt myself drawn in by their warmth and found a spot near where that Lindsay girl had been sitting. She seemed really nice. Yet this was such an unexpected destination. A series of unforeseeable events had brought me here. Was this the purpose of it all? Had I been directed here? They were all genuinely talking about God like he was real to them. Is it possible that the divine had guided me despite all my carefully laid plans? Was there meaning underlying this and everything else that had happened to me in the past two weeks? It was beginning to blow my mind!

I was beyond curious now. I needed to find the answer.

The Next Morning

It was after breakfast when this recently converted Jew from New York named Barry approached me. I could tell by his enthusiasm that he wanted to share some more about Jesus with me. Lindsay and I had talked for over an hour before bed. My understanding of God and Jesus felt like it had just exploded over night. It was all making sense. Like the pot at the end of a rainbow. The destination at the end of a long journey, something in me knew this was what had been drawing me across the country. This God had been pursuing me!

"Would you like to pray with me, Nancy?"

Suddenly it was as if Jesus had made Himself so irresistible to me I could not say a word, but neither could I hold back.

"Yes!"

I prayed the simplest prayer and it felt unreal. Was that all there was to it? A well of emotion rose up. How was this happening? I couldn't comprehend that what they were telling me was true. All I had to do was believe. It had been God that was the strange power that had so recently taken control of my life. Smacking me upside the head with so many wonderful, unexpected, things.

"Nancy, do you want to go to Tuesday women's Bible study at Faith Center with us?" Linda, another sweet woman that lived in the house asked.

"Sure!"

I was eager to learn all I could from these people. I thanked Barry and went to put on my shoes.

The Next Day

This long bearded guy named Erik Sampson washed the dishes with me as I processed my second full day in this house, my new faith, and my upcoming decision on whether or not to stay. We'd gone to Faith Center again this morning for another Bible study and I'd heard Pastor Roy speak words that came to life inside me. Almost as if the Lord was talking to me through them. Lindsay had given me my own Bible yesterday and I'd read through so many chapters of it this morning during their daily quiet time. I was struggling with understanding my faith was real. That really all I had to do was believe in Jesus Christ the son of God and love Him and my new brothers and sisters.

They really did feel like that. Like I was part of their family, participating from within instead of observing from the outside. They'd welcomed me in with open arms. I'd wept so much this morning at that Bible study. The emotions this experience in faith was bringing out of me was overwhelming. I had never experienced a love like I saw in these Christians. It was overflowing and washing me away with it. My three nights were up tonight. Barry and John didn't think I should go but rather move into the house for the three month commitment they required.

Erik had spent the first half part of our dish cleaning duty listening to my story and inner turmoil. Now what? What was my new life supposed to look like? Was I really going to be "different" in a good way? With the wisdom of a mature believer he said, "Just stay focused on Jesus. Keep your eyes on him."

He was right. I wasn't alone anymore. God was with me...He had changed the script of my life and wrote me into His grand story. He'd led me here-- I couldn't deny it. I knew He'd stay with me. I knew He'd keep on leading me.

The Next Day - Greyhound Bus Station

I reluctantly let go of Lindsay and our parting embrace. She had graciously walked me to the bus station. I was headed back on the road, transformed but dying a little inside, leaving such dear new brothers and sisters in Christ behind. God was the one in control of my life now. I was certain I didn't want the reins again.

I climbed the steps of the bus and looked back at Lindsay with her big eyes full of compassion towards me one last time. She was still there watching me get on.

"I love you with the love of the Lord." A new song I'd learned these past few days rose in her voice towards me.

"I love you Lord, and I love my new family!" I said as I waved a final goodbye.

I clutched my new Bible to my chest as I took a seat. Bless them all and praise to you God as my journey continues. You brought me out here all on my own with no friends and then steered me right into a trap of your love. My parents might think I've gone off the deep end. Sue is not going to believe this. Sam is not going to believe this. Not in a million years. I chuckled a little and went to grab my journal to write down the updates of the past day.

> *You saw me before I was born and*
> *scheduled each day of my life before*
> *I began to breathe. Every day was*
> *recorded in your book!*
> **Psalm 139:16 (TLB)**

> *For He has rescued us from the domin-*
> *ion of darkness and brought us into*
> *the Kingdom of the Son He loves, in*
> *whom we have redemption, the for-*
> *giveness of sin.*
> **Col. 1:13-14 (NIV)**

Nancy returned to her home in Michigan and shared her new faith with family and friends. The pastor at her church asked her to share her testimony. As she finished her degree at Michigan State she got involved with Campus Crusade and ran into two friends from her party days that had also gotten saved. Her high school sweetheart Sam also became a believer and they eventually married. They moved states a couple times and as a stay-at-home mom to their two daughters, Nancy has served in various leadership positions in church, Bible Study Fellowship and MOPS. She especially loves telling preschoolers about Jesus. She and Sam currently reside in Cincinnati, Ohio where they worship and serve at Kenwood Baptist Church and have six grandchildren who love and serve Jesus! In the summer of 2023 Nancy had a "spontaneous, random thought" to do a Google search for Liberation House in Eugene and found the video Riley and Carissa had done about the Volume 1 book. When she heard them mention Riley's wife, Lindsay, her heart leaped!!! My Lindsay?? She got the book and reached out, reconnecting with people from Lib house like Lindsay for the first time in almost fifty years! She has reflected often on her amazing journey and the experience at Liberation house where she was encountered by the living God. She is looking forward to retracing her spiritual road trip in October 2025 for her 50th spiritual birthday.

From Nancy: I hope that in reading this miraculous story, "that you may believe that Jesus is the Messiah, the Son of God, and that by believing you may have life in His name." John 20:3

You can read Erik and Linda Sampson's stories in chapters 12 & 13 respectively. You can read Lindsay's story in Becoming Jesus People Volume 1.[1]

Sam and Nancy 1972 dating.

Nancy on the left with friends at a Campus Crusade convention in 1975

---

1. Carissa Gobble and Riley Taylor, "Becoming Jesus People:True Stories of How Love Broke Through In The Jesus People Movement," (GPC Publishing, 2023), 133-140.

Chapter 15

Is This all There is?

Kip's Story

1970 - Eugene Oregon

"Drink, drink, drink, drink!" I refilled my red cup from the keg in the kitchen as my football teammates played a drinking game in the other room. The parents of one of the junior players on the team were out of town and that meant a party and sleepover opportunity. This was the life. The dream of a high school senior! No rules. No adults to tell us what to do. A terrific game last night and now to celebrate. But why was I so bored? Was there anything else in life beyond this? How does it get better than this? What else was there beyond having fun and getting drunk? I wasn't into the drug scene like Mel and Harry were.

I walked down the hall from the kitchen staring at the family pictures on the wall, distancing myself from the noise. A large book with people's faces on it caught my eye on the credenza in front of me. I put my drink down and picked it up. THE WAY was all the clue the title could give me. I opened it up.

It was a Bible!!

What on earth?

I flipped through the pages and was shocked to see words I could understand. I don't think I'd actually read a Bible before. My family was nominally Mormon at best and I never liked the few temple visits we'd done growing up. Thankfully Dad and his alcoholic ways hadn't been really into it either or I would've suffered more religious garbage growing up.

I sat down on a high wingback floral chair further down the hallway and began to read this oddly covered holy book. The words seemed to jump off the page at me. Promises. Hope was in here. How had I never heard about this before?

"Kip! We gotta get to bed man." Our host shook me out of my focus on the pages in front of me. I looked at my watch. It was three in the morning! Had I really been sitting here for three hours reading this? I jumped out of the chair, replacing the book where I'd found it.

February 1971 - South Eugene High School (One Year Later)

"Do you want to ask Jesus to be your savior Kip?" Coach Powell asked me. The residual smell of soap from the showers and sweat on the dirty football jerseys in the corner laundry basket made for an interesting locker room Bible study environment. But we'd just been reading *The Late Great Planet Earth* together and so much of it had struck a chord with my aimless heart searching for something real and significant. Coach Powell had started a chapter of the Fellowship of Christian Athletes and I'd jumped at the chance to learn more about the Bible after that party a few months ago where I'd read words that felt like life.

"Yes. I think I do, coach." I responded.

"Pray with me." He bowed his head and closed his eyes.

I repeated the prayer he spoke word for word. And I felt like I was on cloud nine!

"You're beaming, Kip!" Coach observed as I smiled at him after the prayer ended.

"I feel like I have a purpose now, Coach!"

"That you do son. That you do!" He slapped my shoulder.

I grabbed my books and headed towards my car.

It was dark but inside I felt like I held a light.

I made my way down Willamette St and felt like there was nothing impossible. Any door was open to me. With Jesus as my Lord there was a purpose to life and living I'd never felt before. The light was green when I came to it. Mirroring what I felt like inside. An opportunity to go forward. Nothing stopping me.

The next light was green too!

And the next!

I got home not having been stopped by a red light once. How does that even happen?!

It doesn't...

God. Thank you...

1974 - Faith Center - Eugene Oregon (Three Years Later)

I was the only man in attendance at today's late morning Bible study other than pastor Roy Hicks Jr. who led it. I couldn't get enough of his teaching. I didn't care that I was so out of place among all these ladies. I took the collection cup for childcare his wife Kay passed me and then passed it on to the woman to my right.

"If you want to know what God looks like, it looks like people loving each other." Roy finished his message. I could resonate with that. The less formal structure in this church was attractive compared to my coach's church I'd first gone to. I was making so many real friends here. I'd come to Faith Center because that's where those previous druggie classmates Mel Terry and Harry Lasgaurd had gone. It was a little strange I ended up here when so many of my other athlete friends went to

First Baptist. But Roy had a way of explaining the Bible in such practical terms and bringing everything back to Jesus.

Jesus was my whole life now. Soon after my salvation experience with my coach I'd found that the parties just didn't feel right. I'd go and then realize this is not what God's children do. I just didn't do that kind of thing anymore. But I'd lost a lot of friends because of my change in lifestyle. Almost as if I wasn't friend material if I wouldn't do what they were doing or think the way they thought anymore.

I didn't miss it at all. I was hungry for whatever I could learn from Roy and the people in this church. Steve Overman and I had gotten baptized a year or so ago by Roy in a makeshift baptismal and I'd gotten involved with Campus Life. How could I not pass on and share what I was learning to other young students!

I walked up to Roy as the women all filed out of the worship center to collect their toddlers.

"Hey Roy, I really want to get more involved in church. I really want to learn more."

"Hey Kip. I've been hearing all about your great Campus Life groups you're running. Why don't you go hang out with Joe Wittwer. You can lend him a hand with the youth at church."

"Ya that sounds great."

"Also you should go check out Noel Campbell's Bible study too." He gave me a knowing smile as the estrogen dominating the Wednesday morning Bible studies wasn't lost on him either. "I'm thinking of starting up something for guys like you wanting to learn more. Maybe a ministry school or something. I'll keep you posted. But start with Joe. I think you'll learn a lot with him."

"I'll chat with him Sunday!" I said excitedly.

Any opportunity I could get to learn more I was going to jump on.

"Thanks Roy!"

"See ya Sunday Kip."

1977 - McKenzie River Highway OR-126 - Eugene, Oregon (Three Years Later)

Roy zoomed around the corner in his Porsche 924 at seventy miles an hour on Highway 126 passing a cop car parked on our right.

"Uh, oh." I let slip out of my mouth.

"I know that guy." Roy said as he continued to speed around the next few steep curves. We heard the sirens start up behind us half a mile back.

Had my pastor really just broken the speed limit and kept driving?!

"I'm submitted to the law Kip. If I get a ticket I get a ticket."

We rounded a few more curves until we found a space to pull over and wait for the officer to catch up with us. I recalled a conference we'd gone to a year or so ago when Roy had told us not to mention our card games we'd be playing late that night because the other pastors in attendance didn't believe in doing that kind of thing. They didn't think going to the movies was ok either. It was a different style of Christian leadership and Roy didn't feel a need to pick a fight over it. Just like he wasn't going to pick a fight with this officer of the law.

The sirens got louder and we looked behind us as the black and white sedan with flashing lights sped around the corner going eighty and rushed right past us out of sight.

"He'll be back." Roy said calmly.

I was amazed at my pastor's resolve to roll with the authorities and take the consequences of his actions. He wasn't always this calm in clashes of authority though. I recalled a few months ago when the musical artist Keith Green had come to visit again and over-hearing Roy tell him not to rebuke his congregation as Keith routinely did everywhere he went. "That's my job," Roy had told him. Keith had ignored Roy's request and I knew he wasn't going to be asked back. Roy was protective of his church and congregation. I appreciated when he took stands like that.

The cop came back into view pulling off on the opposite side of the road. I also appreciated what my pastor was modeling for me.

Submission to authority. Not something that was appreciated much in my generation's culture.

1981 - Faith Center - Eugene, Oregon (Four Years Later)

I sat alone on the carpeted floor of the sanctuasium an hour before the Sunday evening service. There was a presence here full of anticipation. As if God himself was waiting in expectation for the people He was going to encounter. We were here to meet with Jesus. I was leading worship tonight for the last time.

"How can I make room for you to move tonight, God?" I prayed aloud.

My wife, Pam, our one year old son Jeff and I were headed to Pullman, Washington in a few weeks. It was time to go. Many others had been sent out before us and we'd known it was coming. There was something God had for us there. Something He wanted to do. A bigger purpose.

The doors opened and I stood up to greet the rest of the worship team as they came in. It was going to be a bitter sweet night.

We practiced the set and I was grateful Roy didn't pull a, "I think Jesus wants to go in a different direction tonight," and make all my practice and preparation go to naught. The service followed a typical but powerful pattern and at the end of the night I repositioned the microphone stand for the last time.

I heard sobbing behind me and turned around.

A woman stood there at the bottom of the little steps to the stage, tears streaming down her face staring at me.

"This is my first time here."

I put my mic down and stepped off the stage. God, what do you want to do in this moment?

Something was clearly happening here.

"I've been deaf from birth and the Lord opened my hearing tonight," she explained, and my heart caught in my throat. Was it possible? Of course it was. People got healed all the time.

"Your music. Thank you."

Now my eyes were filling with tears.

"Praise Jesus." I managed to mutter through the emotion welling up inside me.

I gave her a hug and she left.

I held back the tears as best I could as I collected my raincoat from my seat.

God. You're amazing.

I couldn't have imagined a more perfect parting testimony from this place.

Thank you Jesus.

Thank you.

Therefore, my beloved brethren,
be steadfast, immovable, always
abounding in the work of the Lord,
knowing that your labor is not in
vain in the Lord.
1 Corinthians 15:58 NKJV

A few weeks later Kip and his family went to plant a church in Pullman, WA. The Lord blessed their efforts and the church grew. Four years later they felt the call again to move and they took over a small church in West Linn, Oregon which is now called SouthLake Church and they still serve there today as lead pastors. This small church grew to 2500 in weekly attendance and helped launch a church school partnership movement that was depicted in the award winning documentary film Undivided.[1] Their son Jeff serves as executive pastor at SouthLake. Kip & Pam have four grandchildren. To this day Kip refers to many maxims that Roy shared over their formative years in the faith at Eugene Faith Center.

The following chapter is Pam's story.

Kip Jacob on left at high school bible study.

---

1. Sam Marton, Undivided (2013; Lightning Strikes Entertainment), Film.

Chapter 16

I've Been Praying For You

Pam's Story

Spring 1971 - South Eugene High School

Harry Laserguard's custom t-shirt caught my eye and those of my girlfriends as we gathered around our lockers, getting ready for second period. JE-SUS SAVES it read. What on earth did that mean? Harry was typically always strung out on drugs yet now he'd turned Christian? Was he talking about Jesus saving him from drugs or what? I'd never seen anyone in my Episcopalian church wear a shirt like that. My family went to a nice church just like we were part of a nice country club. Jesus on t-shirts wasn't a Christian thing was it?

I closed my beige locker door, twisting the lock to secure it with my free hand. I'd been hearing some of the stories through the grapevine that Harry and Mel Terry had also gotten clean. Which I don't think I would have believed had I not just seen him walk down the hall completely sober.

"Pam did you see that?!" My friend asked as we walked towards our English class.

"Yes! Is he a Christian now?" I asked hoping for more information.

"That's what they say but not like the Christians we are and churches we go to."

We entered the classroom and found our favorite desks. I couldn't shake the feeling these guys whose lives were transforming before my eyes had something I didn't. My gaze drifted out the window as the rest of our senior classmates filed in.

God, if there is something in this, send me somebody to explain it to me.

The bell rang and I pulled out my textbook, refocusing on the task at hand.

Fall 1971 - Oregon State University - Corvallis, Oregon

Ding Dong!

Should I open the door? I was new to this sorority, just getting settled in as a freshman during orientation week at Oregon State. My parents were so proud. I was on a lawyer track and coming from an upper middle class family this felt like the natural next step in life after high school.

Ding Dong. The door rang again. No one was around that I could see. I guess it wouldn't hurt if I answered it.

I opened the door.

Three young college students stood there with smiles on their faces and pamphlets in their hands. "Hi! We are with Campus Crusade for Christ and were wondering if you've heard of the four spiritual laws?" the tallest one asked.

Spiritual laws? Could this be what Harry and Mel had heard about that had changed their lives? A spark of hope kindled in me. I'd been starting to get a bit disillusioned with the party scene. What if this was an answer to my prayer from all those months ago in high school?

"Please come in. I have been praying for someone to come and explain this to me!"

They didn't move, then seeming to understand I was serious and genuine they all filed into the living area.

I listened intently as they shared each law and how we needed Jesus on the throne of our lives. I needed that. I wanted that! I followed their simple prayer word for word.

"Pam, you're part of the family of God now!" They all hugged me and I felt something new.

As they left I couldn't shake the feeling that something was different.

I felt lighter.

I felt hope!

I was different.

No wonder Harry and Mel had changed so much in such a short amount of time.

That was no ordinary prayer.

The door opened again and a bunch of my sorority sisters shuffled through it laughing.

"Hey Pam! We are headed over to the fraternity two doors down for a party tonight. Go get dressed!"

I knew the drill.

Night time was party time.

But I didn't want to go tonight.

I didn't think I wanted to ever go again.

"No I'm going to stay in tonight I think. I'm feeling strange." I came up with the best excuse I could.

They looked at me oddly. As if they were judging me for lack of participation. Hadn't I just partied with them two nights ago when I'd arrived?

"Whatever, Pam. Stay home then."

I would. I would stay home.

Everything was different somehow.

A Few Months Later - Faith Center - Eugene Oregon

I walked nervously into a little chapel on 18th and Cleveland called Faith Center clinging to my boyfriend Kip's arm. He'd promised I'd be fine. I wasn't so sure. Could you really just pick up and go to any church you wanted to? It wasn't like a country club set up where you could only go to the one you were a member of? Baptists went to Baptist churches, Catholics to mass etc. I didn't look like these people. They all were hippies to a T! Halter tops, cut off pants and all. And here I was in my nice skirt and well combed hair and heels. Just like I'd been raised to dress in my white collar family. Would I stand out like a sore thumb?

Kip led me to one of the pews in the back, thankfully not parading his girlfriend further than necessary. He was kind to me. We really got each other. I'd known him briefly in high school. He had been your typical high school jock. Yet here we both were on this transformative journey of discovering a relationship with Jesus. We'd talked for hours about the implications of what we were reading and learning and how different we felt. We both were watching our friend circle shrink because of our lack of participation in the typical college freshman lifestyle activities. I felt ostracized in a way. Almost as if my friends and sorority sisters wouldn't accept me unless I did the things they did. Liked the things they liked. And Kip Jacob had been going through a similar experience.

I sat silently through the entire service afraid to make a wrong move. But as it ended and we turned to leave I was amazed by the camaraderie and love between people that had nothing in common with each other. A lady dressed similar to me was hugging the hippie shoeless girl next to her! What was this place? Could you really look and be any particular way and it didn't matter to God? Did I not have to look and do what everyone else was looking like and doing?

"Kip, I think I love it here," I whispered in his ear as we walked out.

"I know, right?! It's so different! I want you to meet somebody. She reminds me of you. I think you'll like her. Hey Brenda!" He waved to a woman in the parking lot.

"Hey Kip, who's this?" The woman asked as she joined us.

"This is my girlfriend Pam, she's on break from school up at Oregon State."

"It's lovely to meet you Pam!" She offered her hand and I shook it eagerly. I could use a new friend that was into Jesus just like me and she seemed friendly enough!

Fall 1973 - Faith Center - Eugene Oregon (A Year and a Half Later)

I sat in one of the first few seat rows of the new building Faith Center had moved to a year ago after some remodeling. This gym now served as the sanctuary. Pastor Roy was speaking about prayer and our attitudes.

"Pray like it all depends on Jesus and work like it all depends on you." He spoke and I gulped as his eyes landed on me. Please don't call on me... Please don't call on me...

"Pam, would you come up here and share with us about the work you're doing with Young Life right now?"

I hated when he did this. Just called someone out of the crowd. Why had he picked me?! What was I going to say? I still felt new to this. I'd moved back down to Eugene, wanting the friendships like I had with Brenda Berg and the love I felt in this church. An opening had come up with Young Life a friend of mine had previously held, and I'd filled in. Most of the time I'd just repeat to those kids what Roy taught us on Sundays. I was loving it though.

I nervously made my way to the stage and took the mic from Roy. I found Kip's eyes in the crowd smiling with encouragement. We were getting serious. I wouldn't be surprised if we were soul mates. There was a connection there unlike I'd had with any other guy.

I fumbled through a few testimonies I could think of then hurriedly sat back down in the crowd. I'd survived. Brenda would be proud I'm sure. She'd sort of taken me under her wing and was teaching me how to lead Bible studies and worship. I was learning so much from just being here. How to apply the word of God practically in my life and also getting closer to Him. Even my mind was getting renewed. I was thinking about things more clearly.

The service ended, and Kip and I headed for the hallway exit with the rest of the crowd, but Roy stopped us before we made it under the basket ball hoop.

Oh no.

There's a correction coming I'm sure.

I fumbled my way through that spontaneous sharing time terribly! Why had he called on me?!

"Hey Pam, thanks for sharing with us today."

"Ya, you're welcome."

"You know I just had to tell you I see you speaking to people some day. I think there is a calling on your life. I just see you in front of hundreds of people sharing Jesus with them. God is doing something in you, Pam. It's really great." He gave me a smile then turned to greet a family that was eagerly waiting to speak with him.

I walked down the cement block hallway back to the car with Kip in total shocked silence.

Me? Speak in front of hundreds? Was there really a calling like that on my life?

Jesus, only if you will it.

Only if you will it.

1975 - Fireside Room Staff Dinner - Eugene Oregon (Two Years Later)

"And this is Kip and Pat Jacob," Roy introduced us and I tried not to react to him getting my name wrong. Nobody said anything but I could tell Kay caught the oops. Roy went on to introduce the rest of the Faith Center staff members, and then we blessed the food and made our way around to the buffet table set up opposite the fireplace near the kitchenette. The food was delicious and the company even better as we mingled in this basement-like room called the fireside room. Kip and I had both grown so much in our faith here at Faith Center.

"Pam." I turned around to see a concerned Roy behind me, his wife Kay in the distance shaking her head with a smile. She'd corrected him privately I guessed.

"Would you please forgive me?" He asked, referring to how he'd messed up my name earlier.

"Ray, just don't give it another thought." I said sincerely not trying to laugh at my intentional mispronunciation of his own name.

"No, I need you to forgive me." He took a step closer, no laughter on his face.

I wasn't ready to let the opportunity to rub it in go just yet.

"I forgive you, Ray. Don't worry about it." My husband visibly cringed; he was probably nervous that his new bride was bold enough to joke with the pastor.

Roy took my hand and looked at me intently, still not acknowledging my joke but then a knowing smile spread across his face, "I need to have you forgive me."

"Yes Roy, it's all good." I laughed and he nodded his thanks before returning to Kay across the room.

Kip shook his head and laughed with me. Probably glad the joke had gone over so well. Just the other day we'd been talking about how Roy didn't lower himself to other people's insecurities. He carried an authority and humility that we'd never seen before and we were watching the people around us all benefit from it. I sure hoped and prayed that when it was time to become a mother I'd have some of these wonderful women in this church around me to lean on and learn from. Even if it was just for one year. I had a feeling this wasn't our end all be all home. Both Kip and I had sensed there'd be a day we would need to move on and take what we'd learned to plant another church somewhere. Roy was always talking about how he didn't pay us much because he didn't want us to get comfortable. He wanted us to go out and do the great commission stuff. Fly the nest so to speak.

We would leave the nest at some point I was sure, but for now, I was content. As I looked around the room at all the couples and soon to be couples on staff I couldn't help but feel like I was part of something incredible. A family.

Keep your heart with all vigilance, for
from it flow the springs of life
Proverbs 4:23 ESV

The Lord answered Pam's prayer again and they were at Faith Center the entire first year of their child's life, gleaning wisdom from seasoned parents. In 1981 Pam and Kip and their one year old went to plant a church in Pullman, Washington. The lord blessed their efforts and the church grew. Four years later they felt the call again and they took over a small church in West Linn, Oregon which is now called SouthLake Church, where they still serve today as lead pastors. They now have four grandchildren. Their son Jeff serves as executive pastor at SouthLake as well. This small church grew to 2500 in weekly attendance and helped launch a church school partnership movement that was depicted in the award winning documentary film

Undivided.[1] Pam is thankful that she knew before she was married she was called to the ministry. Roy's prophetic word over her life has come to pass many times over. She speaks at conferences and continues to follow the call to minister in the local church. Recently she got to pray for a girl with spina bifida and watch Jesus heal her.

Pam Jacob at her wedding in sanctuasium.

Kip & Pam's Wedding in sanctuasium.

---

1. Ibid.

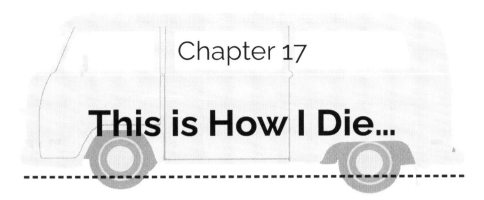

Chapter 17
This is How I Die...

Thomas's Story

1979 - Oregon Highway - Bend, Oregon

We were late to work. My friend Ruse swerved around a hairpin turn going seventy miles an hour in his 58 Studebaker pickup truck. There was a car in the other lane and he swerved again as I grabbed the door handle to brace myself. We missed the car but flew off the road down an embankment and a large boulder stared us in the face. My heart stopped as we collided with the stone and the truck took air. Time stood still. I was going to die.

I was flying now, out the passenger door, in slow motion, and memories from my short life began to filter through my brain. My siblings playing the meanest pranks, the crash of something breaking in Mom and Dad's room as they argued, my older sibs going through their Native American hippie phase with names like Smoking Fox, Moon Feather, and Tobacco Beaver, blowing pipe smoke in my face and getting me high. Those same siblings getting my dog high by putting a pot smoke filled plastic bag over his head. Then them getting saved and turning Christian. Asking my mom the question, "Do you think it's real? What David, Karen, and Lindsay are talking about now? God? Jesus?" while we did the dishes in the kitchen one day. Kneeling by my bed as my sister Karen led me in a salvation prayer when I was sixteen and feeling this love enter my heart I'd never known before.

I saw the boulder go by as I still hung mid air, the truck flipping over in a 360 and Ruse nowhere in sight. This was really it. I wasn't going to survive this fall. More memories flooded in. My friend Brice pulling out a Bible the day after my salvation and me thinking he was into this faith stuff too, only to watch him pull out weed from a cut out hidden compartment inside the book. "Only thing this book is good for, Tom, is hiding dope from our parents." I'd gotten high with him and felt guilty about it. Drugs always made me feel guilty after that. I'd ditched the Christianity interest since I wanted to have fun. Memories of my high school football games came next. The girls, the drugs, the parties. Injuring my back while skiing after moving here to Bend a few months ago. The back brace I'd opted for instead of surgery.

Was I on the ground now? How had I gotten here? I didn't feel myself hit the ground? My focus shifted to the truck landing and careening towards me. My broken vertebrae wouldn't have survived that landing and my body wasn't going to survive this truck. There was a right way to go in life and a wrong way to go in life. I had chosen wrong. I closed my eyes, not wanting to see the impact.

SCREECH!

Nothing happened.

I opened my eyes. The truck was inches away, stuck a quarter turn from making me roadkill.

I was alive.

My breath rushed back into my lungs.

I hadn't died!

Tom, if you had died just now, I would have received you into My Kingdom, a voice filtered through my mind, where all the images had been moments ago, replacing them with one single memory. Me on my knees asking Jesus to be Lord and Savior of my life.

Guilt slammed my chest where no other pain had been from the fall.

"Oh Jesus, I would've hated to have died just now and not have served you with my whole life..." I groaned. How could it be?! I'd done nothing for Jesus! I'd lived my own life my own way despite my promise to him. How could he have accepted me after all of that?!

I wanted to cry but was holding myself rigid, not wanting to make anything worse that could've broken in the crash. Steam from the truck's evaporator was drifting to the sky and I heard distant sirens.

The paramedics arrived and I warned them about my bad back. They scooped me up on some board and transported me to the nearest emergency room. At the hospital three doctors came up to my bed with stunned expressions.

"Thomas, we know you had a ski injury and we've done head to toe X-rays and scans. There's nothing. Your back is completely fine. You are completely fine. You didn't hit anything. We don't know how you're fine but you are."

They left me in my own stunned silence. I got up out of the hospital bed to test out their science and there was no pain. What?! I bent my back in ways it hadn't been able to before the accident. Full range of motion. I was really fine!

Jesus.

Jesus had saved me.

I peeked out my door to be sure there wasn't any nurse or doctor to see my escape. The coast was clear. I walked down the hall and spotted Ruse, with too many bandages and braces to count. He was alive at least, but how could I be walking out of here and he was a bundled up mess of fractures, punctures, concussion, and sprains! I looked away. I needed to do something. My brain wasn't making sense of this right now.

I found my way to the gift shop downstairs and bought a cross necklace. As I put it around my neck I knew I couldn't ever deny God had done something here. He'd spared me. He'd saved me. I needed to acknowledge this.

The Next Day

"Did you guys hear about that car wreck yesterday!" The telephone repairman in his hard hat asked me and my friend as we walked by. Suddenly I held a sense of pride.

"Did I hear about it? Man, I was IN that accident!" I grinned, enjoying my moment of fame.

His eyes locked with mine unimpressed, "Well, I hope you thank Jesus Christ that you're alive right now because he saved your life yesterday. And there's a lot of people in this town that love you. They're praying for you."

"Yes, I thanked him." My hand reached for the new cross at my neck as my friend stared at me awkwardly. We walked on and I was happy to leave the preachy repair guy behind. What was happening to me? My life was spared but now what? We entered my friend's place and he pulled out some LSD. It was like a habit. Muscle memory took over. I took at least four hits.

Rainbows danced in front of me only a few moments later. My friend was out on the couch or a drifting cloud I couldn't tell. I felt myself moving. The panic of the accident and my inner turmoil at being spared a roadkill death had vanished. This was not the greatest trip though I was seriously confused. I think I'm outside?

A pretty light in the distance turned into a brighter light. I was mesmerized. Was that more rainbows? They're so pretty! It was getting bigger. I started walking towards it. I loved rainbows. They made me happy. But maybe I shouldn't get right in front of it. I took a step back.

Whoosh! HONK!

I fell back on my hindquarters and was brought back to reality for a minute. It wasn't a rainbow, it was a car! I'd almost walked into a car on the road! I'd almost died again!!! I looked for a street sign but it was swimming like a fish in the air. Wait, I recognized most of the letters. I was almost home. I stumbled my way forward. Found a door knob that seemed to slip through my fingers a few times but my key worked. I crawled in and shut it. Collapsing on my bed I felt like I was sinking and the ceiling swirling. I should have stuck with two hits, not four. What was I thinking...

Go to Eugene and see your brother David. That voice was in my head again. The same one from the accident.

"Why would I want to do that? He's a Christian. I don't like Christians." I tried to argue with the voice as I drifted off to sleep.

The Next Morning

I looked through the mess on my dresser frantically. I had to go to Eugene and see David but I couldn't find my watch! The Seiko one my grandmother had given me that was worth over a hundred dollars! There's no way I could go back to see my family and have lost that watch! I had to wear it! I caught my own disheveled, long hair reflection in the mirror.

"Who are you?" I barely recognized myself. I turned my gaze to the ceiling. "God! If you help me find my watch I promise I will serve you for the rest of my life!" I was desperate.

Your watch is in the back left pocket of your jeans at the bottom of the dirty clothes hamper.

That same voice from last night and the car accident ran through my mind. I scrambled over to my closet and dug through my hamper, finding the jeans. I put my hand in the back pocket and my jaw dropped. It was there. My watch was right where that little voice in my head had said it was!

A Few Days Later - BlueGrass Music Festival - Eugene, Oregon

The melodies reverberated through the speakers over Pete Taylor and me as we lay out on the grass soaking in the tunes. Pete was my brother in law. My sister Lindsay had married his brother Riley after meeting at that weird Jesus freak commune they called Liberation House. Our two families had known each other a bit growing up. He was a good friend, although he was here sharing with me these things about the end of the world and Jesus coming back that I'd never heard about before.

I had woken up from that acid trip a few days ago not able to shake the feeling I needed to go see my brother David. I'd seen a flier for this festival and thought it was as good of an excuse as any to make the trip down here. David had been happy to see me and found out Pete was going to the same festival. The music was amazing.

"You should read it, Thomas. It was an eye opening book." Pete finished his long tirade.

"What's it called?"

"The Late Great Planet Earth."

The Next Day - Faith Center

"If you're here today and you just know it's time to give up and surrender to Jesus would you raise your hand?" Steve Overman asked from the pulpit after the prophet guy Dick Mills had finished his message. David had brought me to his church this morning and I knew this was it. I was here to get right with God. I closed my eyes and lifted my hand. Nothing happened. I opened them again and a man that had been prophesying earlier, Dick, was staring at me. I started to pull

my hand down but he grabbed it, closed his eyes, bowed his head and prayed with me
.

Something started tingling in the hand he held. It was getting hotter. My whole arm was warming up now like something was pushing its way into my body. It was in my shoulders now. I was almost trembling. This was not a drug trip! I hadn't had any drugs since almost walking into that oncoming car in Bend! My whole body was overcome by this feeling I couldn't explain. But something was missing.

The darkness wasn't there.

The sadness wasn't there.

The depression wasn't there.

Instead I felt something else. Peace. I lost my breath for a moment and met Dick's eyes.

"It's alright. Everything's gonna be okay." His words soothed the question in my soul of whether I would live or die. Take the right path or the wrong. It was done now. I was surrendered. I had made it. God had miraculously saved me not once but twice in the span of a week and now here I was washed in His mercy. Covered by His grace. The colors around me seemed brighter somehow. This was it. I'd chosen Jesus.

Three Days Later

Water still dripped down my legs and neck from my soaked clothes and hair but I didn't care. The sun was setting and everything was magically golden as I walked back to the other part of Faith Center to change, post baptism. The parking lot was full of cars but empty. I took a little twirl and waved my damp towel in the air. I was free! I felt like I'd just had everything in my past washed away. I jumped in the air! The sun's final rays created a magical atmosphere outside that mimicked what I felt inside. I got it now. What had changed my siblings so dramatically all those years ago. It was this. It was Jesus! I danced my way to the other building. I wasn't just spared from death. I was alive!

1981 - Jacobs Family Home - Eugene, Oregon (Two Years Later)

Kip Jacob was leaving. I wracked my brain for what I was going to say when the turn got to me in this goodbye gathering. What was I going to say about him? Would I share my gratitude for how he'd been my mentor? How much I enjoyed the milkshake meet ups to talk about Jesus with this guy that was one of the Faith Center youth pastors? What about the dinners at his house he'd invited me over for? Or the copious amounts of time he'd just spent with me? I couldn't decide.

I was living at Liberation House now. I'd decided I needed to go through their program a few months ago. Even though my first year as a Christian I'd grown so much from just Kip's mentoring, and my own brother David's, I'd been hungry for more. I remembered my walk with Dan Purkey and how he'd mentioned that my first year had been kind of the honeymoon season of my faith and now I was walking into a new season, a season of learning the disciplines of my faith, of character building and that Lib House was going to help with that. And it really was. It had humbled me. I was learning so much.

A guy three people down on my left was holding back tears as he shared about Kip. It was almost my turn. What was I going to say? Would I be able to say anything without crying!

Kip locked eyes with me and smiled. But they weren't Kip's eyes looking at me. They were Jesus' eyes. This was what Jesus looked like. Jesus looked like the guy that would take me out to milkshakes. Sure, it had been Kip, but I didn't see Kip right now. I saw Jesus loving me through a real human person. Jesus spending time with me. Jesus saying *come over and have dinner with me*. The love in those eyes was breaking my heart. The tears welled up and I dashed out of the living room. I couldn't stay there. I'd just be a basket case! I'd see Kip on his last Sunday service tomorrow and share with him then.

I bounded down the porch steps to the street. I continued to a nearby park and collapsed on a swing and let the tears fall freely in private. Jesus had saved me and not just my life but my spirit too. Then he'd loved me through the hands and feet of the people in this place. I'd grown up. I'd been instantly delivered of all addictions that night I'd prayed with Dick Mills. I was a completely different person. This love that was so profound and I didn't deserve was here to stay. I saw Kip's eyes again, mirroring the love of my Jesus. My Jesus. The one that knew me intimately.

"That's what I want to do," I spoke out-loud through the tears and snot that streamed down my face. "I want people to see Jesus in me like that and know," I caught a breath between sobs, "that people will know that you love them."

That warm presence I'd come to recognize as the Holy Spirit settled on me. He saw me. He saw my heart and my hopes. He'd been guiding me all this time. If I could just help one person come to know this love too and see Jesus in me. That's all I wanted in this life. That's the path I wanted to go down now. That was the right way to live a ransomed life that had been given a second chance. A life full of loving God and sharing it with others.

A Few Weeks Later

This place felt like family now. All of us hundreds of people crammed into this repurposed gym. Roy was finishing his message. He was the best Bible teacher I'd ever heard.

"If any of you want to come and just present yourselves to the Lord in response you can come down to the front." He gave an invitation and I accepted, along with at least a hundred other people. His message had connected with me at such a deep level. I raised my hands in surrender with my brothers and sisters surrounding me.

"I have a word." Roy continued, and I closed my eyes. "It's not for everybody. It's for one person, maybe two. The Lord says, I have seen your tears and I know the difference between tears of joy and tears of sadness and your tears of joy at wanting to serve me are gonna be like seeds that bring forth a great harvest of souls." My hands dropped to my heart and the tears came again. The memory of my prayer and weeping on the swing a few weeks ago flashed before me. God really had heard me! This word of Roy's was His answer. He had seen me on that swing and heard my prayer to be used by Him. I fell to my knees under the significance of it all. This sold out life for Jesus was blowing my mind and capturing my heart in ways I was only barely beginning to understand.

"Thank you Jesus." I whispered through my tears. "Thank you."

> *But thanks be to God, who always*
> *leads us in triumph in Christ, and*
> *through us reveals the fragrance of the*
> *knowledge of Him in every place.*
> **2 Corinthians 2:14 NASB**

Jesus granted Thomas's prayer....he went on to serve in youth ministry and other pastoral roles in Eugene and in churches in Washington State. One of his ministry experiences left him hurt by the church and antagonistic towards organized Christianity. In 2020 during a visit to his siblings in Portland, OR he was convicted of his unforgiveness and bitterness and restored his relationship with Jesus and the church. He found community again at Kairos Church, which was meeting in a barn at the time, and ran into friends from his Faith Center days. He still attends Kairos and his passion for Jesus has never been stronger. Because of his faith transformation recently his daughter has also come back to her Jesus and their family is healing. The years the bitterness stole from him are being restored. Thomas has four kids. He continues to share his testimony with others and proclaim the graciousness of God in his life.

You can read Thomas's siblings David and Lindsay's testimonies, and Dan Purkey's story, in Volume 1 of Becoming Jesus People.[1]

Lib house, Thomas in center of bottom row.

Thomas

Chapter 18

Drugs in the Bible

David's Story

Winter 1971 - Eugene Oregon

The semi-safety of Lawrence street in Eugene, Oregon seemed to be a safe place to park my 1964 Ford Econoline hippie van, full of drugs stashed in the nooks and crannies of its hull. I was home. The level of fear and paranoia I lived with daily calmed down about fifty percent. I still had to get all this cash crammed in my overall pockets into the house and tomorrow to the bank. I wasn't safe yet. I looked in all my mirrors to be sure there wasn't anyone lurking around the house ready to jump me. My uncle had taught me my senior year of high school to, "never trust a doper." Thus the massive amount of cash I always had on hand as a drug dealer. "Never take credit David. They'll never pay you back," he'd told me. He hadn't told me the constant level of anxiety that accompanied carrying around dozens of Ben Franklins.

The coast looked clear and I unlocked the van door, quietly stepping outside. Locking it up I gave the handle a tug to be sure the vehicle was secure for the night with its precious cargo hidden inside. I couldn't take any chances. This was my nightly routine after hitting up the rich fraternities on the University of Oregon campus. I had mushrooms, pot, hash, speed, downers, LSD or miscellaneous psychedelics but I drew the line at heroin. Didn't want anything to do with it. I walked around the van checking that all looked normal. The van itself was a huge cop target. It just screamed "pull me over" with its giant sun painted on its side, and no windows but the two in back with curtains and anti-Vietnam war stickers in the windows. My heart would stop every time I'd go by a police car or station or even the university security. I'm sure I was decreasing my life span just from the paranoia I lived under every day.

All the drugs were well hidden during my van inspection so I walked into the house, giving a glance over my shoulder that no one was watching, before quickly slamming the door shut and turning the dead bolt. My brother Dennis, lying wasted on the couch, didn't even flinch. Now I was really home. A relief washed over me. Another successful drug run complete. I tossed my keys onto the kitchen counter and rolled myself a joint. I eased myself into a large overstuffed chair opposite my brother as the effects of the pot started to calm my nerves.

It wasn't just the fear of getting caught, robbed, or jumped that I lived with as a dealer but it was also the threat of war. Dennis snored loudly, having succumbed to sleep after another day of getting stoned and listening to his favorite rock albums. He'd survived the Vietnam war in the Air Force, loading bombs on jet fighters, but not without it leaving a mark on him. I did not want to end up like that. I had a very low draft number and I was on all the waitlists for the ROTC. I was even willing to become a Beaver and go to Oregon State if it meant I could kiss the threat of the draft goodbye. Dennis had survived with his body intact but not his mind and I knew if I got called up I wouldn't make it. Just like the more than half dozen soldiers I assisted in burying as a Catholic altar boy back in high school.

I blew out the smoke from my last joint and took a final swig of wine and closed my eyes. My muscles started to relax more. But the dead faces, at their funerals, of those eight friends my age killed in action still haunted me. I could be the next one. I didn't want to be. I'd taken a year off since high school and moved to this big college town. I'd saved up enough money as a dealer and from working in a plywood mill to pay for college. The English Comp class end of term creative writing paper was due in two days and I had nothing to write about. Nothing.

There was nothing creative in this world. Just fear and uncertainty. I stayed high every moment I could to try and forget how messed up of a world I lived in. My childhood in New York before we'd moved to Oregon also filtered through my mind. I'd been so shocked to see signs as we drove down Interstate 5 to Grants Pass telling all colored folks to be out of town by 5pm. What kind of state had we moved to six years ago? It was mostly the smaller towns like Medford and Grants Pass. I'd been happy to get out of them up here to Eugene and Duck-land. But seriously, our culture was just messed up. I'd never witnessed such racism in New York, where everywhere around me somehow looked different.

The world was crazy. The president couldn't be trusted, the country couldn't be trusted, the people I hung out with REALLY couldn't be trusted. They all knew I had money and what I did. My happy go lucky older brother was just a stoner. What was the point of it anyways? Why was I putting myself through this? Nobody cared. I had no real friends. They just were friends because of the discounts they could get or free dope and booze from me. It was stupid. All of it pointless. It was just me and my drug filled life. Our saying was, "there was no hope without dope".

Why not just end it.

Have some sort of control over how at least my life came to its final moments? Maybe that would make a good paper. I could creatively talk about how I would die and why this place wasn't worth living in anymore.

The Next Day

The dimly lit, back dark corner of the Lane Community College library was comforting and a safe place as I finished up a suicide note I'd turn in as my final paper and final creation in this life. I peered through my rose tinted gold rimmed glasses that had once been my grandmothers at the papers in front of me. The only thing I'd regret was not getting to know Becky from English class more. I'd been shocked when she'd said yes when I'd asked her out after a few weeks into the class. Me in my bozo the clown embroidered overalls and long dark hair had just snagged a date with the cutest chick. Although I'd quickly discovered she hung out with all these Jesus freak friends. I think one of them had warned her about dating me. They'd seen me at all the parties. Probably knew exactly what kind of guy I was. We'd just been casual friends since. But those Jesus people would wave to me around campus. Loretta, Carol, Missy, and even that guy Jim Millard would answer my sarcastic Christianity questions if I ran into them. Well, they might not miss me trying to steal their friend Becky away.

"David." A firm, serious voice called my name.

I looked up from my papers down the aisle of books. No one was there.

"Why won't you give me a chance?" the voice said.

A new kind of fear crept down my spine.

I stood up looking down each aisle within earshot for the owner of the voice.

Nothing, there was no one in sight.

I wasn't high.

I wasn't dead yet.

Was God talking to me?

I sat back down with my paper.

"David, why won't you give me a chance?" The audible voice questioned me again.

I looked up and looked around again as the hair on the back of my neck stood up.

Jesus.

Jesus was talking to me.

I grabbed my bag and rushed out of the building as fast as my legs could carry me. I ignored a few customers outside asking me what I had on me that day and got in my van. Like muscle memory I drove out of the campus to Springfield where I knew that guy Jim Millard lived.

Pulling in Millard's driveway, I turned off the van, the fear of God still propelling me like a magnet to get answers. I knocked and Jim opened the door.

"You won't believe what just happened to me!" I declared.

"Come in David." He showed me in. "This is Bob Schultz my mentor and John Alban my friend from Young Life"

"You guys! Jesus just spoke to me!! I was in the library and then all the sudden this audible voice came out of nowhere saying, 'David why don't you give me a chance?!' There was literally nobody around!" I paced the living room trying to make sense of it all.

"David, do you think God is trying to tell you something?" Jim asked, with a knowing grin on his face.

Yes. I couldn't deny an unexplainable audible voice, with no drugs to blame, that intuitively I knew it was Jesus.

Why don't you give Me a chance...

Ok sure.

"Yes Jim. I do think He's saying something to me but show me in the Bible where it says we can't do drugs? The kinds that God himself created. Organic plants. Where's the verse that says don't do drugs?" I spotted a Bible on the coffee table and shoved it in Jim's lap as the others in the room stared. I didn't care. If this was real, if God was trying to get my attention I needed to know this lifestyle I was living wasn't right in His eyes. Otherwise I wasn't going to change anything.

"Show me where it says I can't get loaded and I'll quit right now!" I shouldn't need any more convincing when voices were calling me out of thin air but this was my life. So it was the line for me. My fleece if you will. If it was in the Bible I'd surrender it all.

March 1972 - Middle of the Georgia Straight - Stormy Canadian Coastline Waters (One Year Later)

The 130 foot yacht lurched again to the port side and the china in the hutch smashed against the glass display windows. This was not how I wanted to die. The whirl of the three coast guard helicopters helping us navigate the straight in the storm reminded me of what our ex British Navy captain had said a few hours ago. "If this ship capsizes we'll all freeze to death in these waters"

Yep, not what I'd signed up for on this spring break work week trip to some Young Life camp in Malibu, Canada. There were 40-50 college kids throwing up in buckets in the ship's dining room and a few crazy Jesus freaks playing their guitars and singing happy Jesus songs. Sheesh, we're all about to die and they're singing, "I've got the joy, joy, joy..." This is crazy! I shakily made my way to my cabin to lie down, bracing myself against the halls as the ship jerked from side to side. I passed Becky's friend's room at the perfect moment to see him retch into a plastic bucket. My own stomach turned. I had to get out of here.

Making it back to the cabin, I laid down on my bunk to try and still the dizzy feeling in my head. I closed my eyes, blindly feeling for the tiny metal film canister I'd brought along in my backpack filled with the most righteous weed. My fingers curled around it and I wanted to pop off the lid and roll myself a joint to take the edge off. But I knew that was too risky.

If this was how I was going to die, I wished I could at least get myself so wasted I wouldn't be able to tell. Why had the overconfident captain chosen today to think he knew a better course? His big commander's ego had convinced him to go right up the middle of the straight vs following single file behind the other five ships hugging the coastline like he was instructed. I just wanted out of this metal coffin!

I wanted to inhale the smoke of the plant that calmed my fears the best. Why hadn't I gone through with my suicide ideas in that paper? Why did this have to be the way I died? I hadn't even wanted to go on this trip! I had saved up and planned to go backpacking in the Olympic National Park and get stoned for a whole week straight. But then the money I'd been expecting didn't arrive and I'd spent my savings on fixing the van so it would safely make the trip north. Becky and her friends had convinced me to go with them instead, and be the driver to Vancouver, where we'd then hopped on this stinking ship. The camp was only accessible by boat or seaplane. What had I gotten myself into?

Jim and his friends hadn't found anything in the Bible that day a few months ago to convince me God didn't want me to do drugs. I was so exhausted, I curled up under a sleeping bag, hoping sleep would take me.

The Next Day - Malibu Club Young Life Camp - Malibu, Canada

"I need 15 volunteers to inspect and clean the kayaks," the leader asked at the front of the breakfast room in the lodge. Fifteen hands went up and then filed out of the room to do their volunteer work for the day. Breakfast had been great but I was still so confused why people would want to pay money to get up here just to have to work for four hours of the day every day. Sure the scenery was gorgeous but I wasn't convinced it was worth the dangerous trip we'd endured to get here.

"I need three volunteers to go walk and inspect the water pipeline that feeds the spring water to the camp." A guy to my left with long freaky hair and bib overalls, like I was wearing, raised his hand. A guy to my right with long hair and a leather jacket raised his hand. These were my kind of dudes. My hand shot up in the air.

"Great! You three will need to take the fourteen foot aluminum boat down by the dock to get there." I headed out of the lodge with the other two guys.

Back dropped against clear blue skies, the breathtaking granite rock cliffs that plunged into the still inlet water eased the uncomfortable feeling I'd had a moment ago sitting in the large room of Jesus freaks wanting to work with no pay. This place almost had a magical feel to it. A dusting of snow still capped the highest peaks. The crystal clear blue water mirrored an eagle flying overhead as we three climbed into the boat.

Leather jacket dude navigated down the inlet towards the pipes we were supposed to inspect. Now this was what I had envisioned my spring break being. Out in God's beautiful nature with some narcotics in my system to enhance the experience.

"Hey, do you guys want to get loaded?" I asked as I reached in my jacket pocket for the film canister of contraband.

They stared at me blankly.

"Hold on," I pulled out the small metal canister and held it out for them to see. "I got some righteous weed right here, you guys want to get stoned?"

"No." Leather jacket guy responded.

"We don't do that anymore." Long hair overall guy agreed.

"You don't?" I was confused. "Why?"

"Because the Bible tells us we're not supposed to."

Ya right, no one had been able to show me that before. "Okay then, you show me where it says in the Bible that you can't get loaded."

Leather jacket guy turned to face me fully and grabbed his backpack. He pulled out a JB Phillips New Testament and opened towards the back. "Ok, coming right up, it's in Ephesians 5:18 through 20" He began to read. "Don't get your stimulus from wine (for there is always the danger of excessive drinking), but let the Spirit stimulate your souls. Express your joy in singing among yourselves psalms and hymns and spiritual songs, making music in your hearts for the ears of God! Thank God at all times for everything, in the name of our Lord Jesus Christ."

It hit me like a bolt of lightning to the heart.

Every sense disappeared except the smash of the boat on the water as we continued toward our destination.

"This doesn't just mean wine. It means any kind of stimulus. Anything that you would consume that would move you out of the realm of the Spirit of God." He offered the Bible to me to inspect for myself. But I didn't need it.

I couldn't deny it. God had just showed it clearly to me in His Scriptures.

It was right there.

I understood now, God graciously answering my final question holding me back from surrender.

That Evening

"If you've got any unfinished business with God, now is the time to go be by yourself with Him and take care of it," The Young Life leader said after the evening meeting had finished. "Once you have, come back here." A bunch of people walked out to various halls and I found myself drawn to a bench outside on the peninsula looking over the inlet under the starry night sky, unobstructed by city lights. It was a glorious spot.

I couldn't deny that voice from the library as God seeking me. I couldn't deny He'd just answered my biggest question point blank. It really did say in the Bible not to get high. The canister of weed felt like it was burning a hole in my pocket. I pulled it out.

"Ok God." I looked up at the creation around me declaring the majesty of a creator. A fish jumped out of the water a few feet away. "I'm gonna trust you."

Before I could change my mind I chucked the small metal container as far as I could. It landed with a small splash and the ripples that expanded around it seemed like miniature waves for such a small thing. A weight lifted off of me, I felt free.

I turned and headed back to the lodge. Finding Becky and her friends I filled them in with what had just happened.

"You brought weed up here?!" Becky exclaimed in shock, and shame washed over me.

"That's not important, what is important is we get you connected with Jesus. Will you pray with me David?" One of her friends asked and I nodded my head.

As we finished the prayer my chest filled with emotion. Tears streamed down my face. Something was happening to me. Something was filling me. Love pushed its way past the fear that was dissolving as if a fifty-five gallon drum of God's love was getting poured over me. I hadn't lived without fear in so long it was a strange sensation to be without it. I peered out through my tears at the people around me. They were genuine. Somehow I knew I could trust them. Was this the community I'd been needing? The tears came fast now.

A Week Later - Alton Baker Park on the Willamette River - Eugene, Oregon

I watched the river water rush by. I had bills. I had rent. Electricity, phone, water etc. How was I going to pay for them? Camp had been an emotional mess. It was strange to feel so loved and not be subject to paranoia and anxiety as had been my norm. But now I wasn't in a magical Canadian isolated retreat anymore. I was home and reality was here. Do I keep selling drugs? How will I make a living? How will I survive? I wasn't going to take them but it was my major source of cash flow and income. Becky's determined face flashed before my eyes as I recalled her words a few hours ago when I'd knocked on her door and shared my dilemma with her. "Would Jesus want you to sell that dope?" She'd said simply.

I'd known the answer. There was no question.

I looked down at the big black garbage bag I held with an iron fist. I saw some big rocks near the bank and walked over. This needed to be final. I tossed the rocks in the bag that held all the drugs I could find in my home and van. I'd even found a garbage bag full of them under a seat and realized how much God had protected me from the border patrol coming home from Canada. Becky and two other minors had been in the van on our drive home and if those guards hadn't gotten distracted from some other commotion and waved us through they would've found that bag for sure. I'd forgotten to take it out before we'd left Eugene. Jesus was so merciful to me. Had I been caught with it and minors in the car going over international borders, I'd have gone to prison for a long time.

I rolled the black bag up as tight as I could and tied off a knot.

Here goes nothing.

I tossed it with all my might into the middle of the rushing Willamette river.

"Ok God. I'm going to trust you for my future."

I hopped back in my fixed up hippie van and drove home.

I began to pray the best I knew how. "Okay Jesus, I hope you can come through for me like you protected me on the road trip home but I have no idea what work I can do."

I pulled in the driveway and turned off the ignition. No need to scout the neighborhood anymore. There wasn't anything here worth stealing.

I got out and walked into the house.

"David!" My college roommate Danny's panicked voice met me at the door.

"Where's all the dope? Where is it!"

"I threw it in the Willamette."

"You WHAT! You threw it all in the river, are you freaking crazy! What the hell did they do to your head up there when you went to Canada!?"

"I couldn't sell it, Danny. I don't do that anymore."

"You could've sold it to me!" he pounded his chest dramatically.

"I couldn't sell it to you either man."

"I can't believe you!" he stormed off to his room down the hall.

I needed to get a job.

May 1973 - Faith Center - Eugene, Oregon (One Year Later)

Becky and I made our way down a long cement block corridor with windows lining the right wall. This didn't look like a church but she'd insisted we come try it out because Jim spoke so highly of it. I'd been going to the Newman Center since my return from Canada and getting not one but two jobs within days of throwing those drugs in the river. God had provided even a great four dollar an hour wage for me! But just a few weeks ago we'd gone down to Wolf Creek, Oregon to visit my brother Dennis who had been so depressed he said he couldn't get high anymore. He was talking suicide like I had been just five months ago. My constant daily prayer had been, "God you have to make a way for me to share with Dennis what you've shared with me. I'd even give up my salvation if you'll give me a chance to tell Dennis what you have for him." Then the opportunity had presented itself and Becky and I had shared as best we could with the rudimentary knowledge we had of the Gospel. But Dennis hadn't wanted anything to do with it, he couldn't understand what we were talking about.

Then the next week, on Friday, there was a knock at my front door in the afternoon after school. I'd opened it to find my giant strawberry blond afro brother asking me, "I don't know what you've got bro. But I gotta have it." So the next day I had taken him down to Coos Bay and Sunset Beach State Park and shared the gospel again as best as I could with this burned out previously bomb loading Air

Force veteran. As soon as he'd finished asking Jesus for forgiveness and to be his Lord and Savior a huge surprise wave came up, almost washing us off the rocks! Talk about getting baptized by God himself!

We were planning to get a place together now but Dennis had to go back home to pack up all his things. While he was gone, I was checking out this church with Becky.

From the outside it looked like an old military quonset hut and inside was no better. I was so confused as we found seats with Jim and his friends in the middle of a repurposed gymnasium. Basketball hoops still hung on two sides of it.

A lady was on the piano and a man on the organ and this short brown-haired guy with a navy blue shirt, white tie, and burgundy blazer with white top stitching on the pockets and lapels that sort of matched his white and navy blue houndstooth patterned bell bottom pants and white boots, stood up to give the sermon.

What the heck!

He was talking about love, about faith, about trust and peace.

"Reach across the aisle and grab the hand of the person next to you. Let's pray." The preacher bowed his head and I awkwardly held hands with Becky on my left and a stranger on my right. What in the world was this place! We'd never done anything like this in Catholic mass growing up. This wasn't church! This was sacrilege! This pastor even asked us to break up into small groups of 3 or 4 and pray for each other's needs. These were strangers. I don't know how to pray for strangers. *This was crazy*, I thought.

The prayer ended and Becky and I headed back to my van.

"That was crazy. I'm never going back there again." I declared.

Two Weeks Later - Sunday Evening Service - Faith Center

Cheers erupted around us and echoed through the upside down Noah's ark like ceiling of the gym as another lost soul got baptized in the makeshift baptismal. Total submersion was the trend here I guessed. Again, another thing in total contrast to my Catholic upbringing. I had tried to warn Dennis but he'd had a crazy encounter in Grant's Pass at a meeting with other Christians and come back here totally on fire for Jesus, to the point I was a little jealous. He said he'd been baptized in the Holy Spirit. His energy and boldness and zeal was exciting. He'd been told he should go to Faith Center and I had tried to talk him out of it but here we were. Not for the first time today but a second evening service! Who goes to church twice in one day?

The dude stepped out of the baptismal soaking wet, as the people around me continued to lift up vocal intimate praises to Jesus. These people were genuine. A woman now stepped into the baptismal pool and confessed her faith in Christ. They submerged her and she came up out of the water beaming the biggest smile! Two guys we'd met this morning - Brian O'Grady and Barry Tuckman - with their long hair, let out some whistles and cheers to our right. These guys had been like me. Something was happening here. My older brother was hungry for it. And it was growing on me. They had a fire I wanted to emulate. Maybe I should give this place another chance.

1974 - Love House - Springfield, Oregon (One Year Later)

John Favors was ready to start worship. He plucked at his guitar in our living room as we got ready for Saturday Bible study. But Mike Meeks wasn't there yet..

"You guys go ahead and start, I'll be right back."

I hopped in my van and drove all the way to 8th and Blair street to the druggie house I knew Mike lived in along with Tim Murff and a bunch of other stoners. I knew this house well from my old life. I could make a hundred dollars from this house easily back in the day. I'd even come over and preached hellfire and brimstone to these people. I'd gone down to Grants Pass with my brother to a men's Bible study group at a coffee shop where they laid hands on me and prayed for me to be filled with the Holy Spirit. BAM! The Holy Spirit came into me, I felt the warm fire inside and started praying words I had never heard of before. The men told me I was praying in tongues. That infilling had given me the same boldness I'd seen in Dennis. Even the people at work on lunch breaks would hear messages from me now! No one had responded to those messages. I hadn't been the one to share the gospel with Mike but he had told me he was already saved. He shouldn't still be here. He'd told me he'd come to our Bible study.

I knocked on the door.

Tim Murff answered, hung over and drowsy from a hard night of partying.

"What do you want, Ford...."

"I'm here to get Mike. Where is he?"

"He's down the hall in his bedroom."

I made my way down the hallway and opened the door to his room. He was sound asleep in bed! I yanked the covers off of him. "HEY, GET UP! You're supposed to be at the Bible study right now!"

"Huh?" He blinked open his sleepy eyes.

"Get up. Let's go."

I helped drag him to the van and we both hopped in as he rubbed his eyes and yawned. We'd run into each other earlier in the week and exchanged salvation stories. He came with me that day to Ken Klein's Bible study and I'd invited him to the one at our place on Saturday morning. He needed to get out of that place where he was living.

"Mike, you should come move in with Dennis and me you're starting a new life."

"Ya man. You're probably right."

We drove back to my place and all I could think of was all the people that didn't have a friend to drag them out of a drug house into community fellowship like the kind I'd found in this faith and church. My brother's and my lives were changing right before our eyes. If we could be a safe place for others like us to grow in this new found faith together then I wanted to do what I could to make it happen.

This was community.

This was real friendship.

And getting high on the Most High was better than any other drug I'd ever experienced.

Being confident of this very thing,
that He who has begun a good work
in you will complete it until the day of
Jesus Christ.
Philippians 1:6 (NKJV)

Trust in the Lord with all your heart,
And lean not on your own under-
standing; In all your ways acknowl-
edge Him, And He shall direct your
paths.
Proverbs 3:5-6 (NKJV)

Mike Meeks did move in with David & Dennis. A few weeks later Tim Murff came to the Bible study shocked to find out David Ford had turned Christian. Tim gave his life back to Christ. Mike's older brother Ray came up to stay and participated in a Saturday Bible study at the Ford's place and got saved and he moved in with them too. They outgrew that house in Springfield and moved over to a large five bedroom house in South Eugene Hills. Then Joel Chance, Mike Norval and Ron Provance also moved in after getting saved. Many shenanigans took place but also lots of discipleship. David married Becky in April 1975. In 1986 they moved to the bay area with Ray & Cindy Meeks. They have served in church leadership and nonprofit ministries for decades and now reside in Parker, Colorado working with EKKLESIA Prison Ministry in a level 4 prison once a month. They have two children and three grandchildren.

You can read Mike Meeks' story in chapter 20.

David and Becky his wife

David and his van.

Chapter 19

Vietnam to Oregon

Dennis's Story

December 1968 - Over Thailand/Vietnam Waters

The whirr of the F-4 bomber engine purred in the background as I sulked. "Ford! Get the next payload ready!" I got up off my seat and headed for the ammunition bay. I seemed to always get the short end of the stick in life. Here it was almost Christmas, halfway through my Air Force deployment, and I'd been assigned work today when the famous comedian Bob Hope was visiting our base in Thailand! This was my luck in life. I'd tried to beat the odds of the draft by enlisting in this branch of the armed forces. I was more likely to survive the Vietnam war from the air than on the ground. I'd just graduated from high school after our family had moved us out to Oregon from New York my senior year. I'd only made two other transplanted student friends that year, who'd come from out of state too. I was for sure going to get called up if I'd sat around and gambled with the draft post graduation. I'd even reached out to God, but he apparently hadn't heard me.

"Coming!" I yelled over the monstrous noise this iron bird made. It was like muscle memory, this twelve hour a day job six days a week. I only had ten months left, then I was off to Florida.

April 1973 - Wolf Creek, Oregon (Five Years Later)

I stared at my face in the rusty mirror of the outhouse. My strawberry blond afro filled the frame and my sin weighed heavily on me. I'd gotten reliant on alcohol and cigarettes in the Air Force. I'd had a month off before Florida coming back from the war which gave me time to buy my first car, a 1966 GTO, one hot car to be sure. It had been fun to drive all by myself from Oregon to Florida. I shivered inwardly as I recalled driving through Mississippi and seeing white cloaked ghost-like figures in a field next to a burning cross. I'd gotten out of there as fast as I could! What might have happened if I got stopped by the local Sheriff?!

Life had dragged on these past few years, since I was honorably discharged. I'd had a couple girlfriends. I'd totaled that wonderful new car from late night visits to one of those girlfriends. So, I'd returned to Grants Pass and lived with my parents for a while. But there had been no work, no prospects, and depression had hit full swing. My brother had had the answer to ease my pain. This thing called Mary Jane. Which of course led to harder drugs. It was something I used to squash all the job rejections. I had eventually found a job at the mill, only to get fired. So I had moved to Eugene with my brother David. He worked. I lived off unemployment. We smoked weed, had girlfriends, and were quite happy as long as that lifestyle continued. But unemployment hadn't been enough so my live-in girlfriend and I moved to a place in southern Oregon called Wolf Creek, to take care of a shack of a house being built we could stay in for free. I had no direction in life and no future to look forward to...

My drug hollowed eyes stared back at me in the mirror. I didn't know if I could keep going. What was the point of it anyways. I lived from one drug hit or joint to the next. I was useless. Nobody had work for me. I couldn't even provide a decent living space for my current girlfriend. Here we were out in this hole of a place with an outhouse for a toilet.

I looked away and walked out. I needed to call David.

I was ready to leave this world. I should at least say goodbye.

A Few Days Later - Sunset Beach, Oregon Coast

I took in a big breath of salty ionized air, the hard wet surface of the protruding rock was getting uncomfortable as I read through this card David had left up here with me. It was low tide, so we'd scrambled up this edifice and had taken in the view of the crashing waves. He'd convinced me on my suicidal phone call to meet him and drive to the beach. He'd really changed. He wasn't stoned anymore. He had a life to him I hadn't seen in ages. Hope maybe?

He'd done his best a few minutes ago to explain this new relationship with Jesus he had and his story of what had happened up in Malibu, Canada. I wasn't really sure what to expect with this faith thing but I was willing to give it a shot. I was on the last line of this little instruction card of four spiritual laws. There was a prayer here it said to read out loud.

I could barely hear my own voice over the crashing waves. "He washes my sins away."

WHOOSH! I looked up in time to see the wall of sea water about to drench me.

Bam! The wave wall hit and soaked me to the bone with its cold pacific ocean salt water. What had just happened?! I watched the foam recede and fall down the sides of the boulder. The card was soaked. My clothes were sticking to me and my hair was dripping. Was the tide coming back in?

I stood up to look. Something was different. Through the cold water that stuck to my limbs I felt something new. Like I was clean? No, it was more than that. I was missing the weight and burden of my sin and shame that had overwhelmed me! I'd never even felt this free as a good Catholic altar boy growing up. I wasn't even in a church! I spotted David running towards me on the beach below waving wildly. I made my way down the rock, careful not to slip on its re-wetted surface.

"David!" I caught up with him on the sand. "Did you see that!" I pointed back to the boulder.

"Yes!!! Are you ok?!" He was a little out of breath from his run.

"I'm more than ok, bro! I'm free!" I lifted my hands wide in glee. I didn't care about my ocean baptism and how wet I was. The depression was gone! David rushed into my arms for a bear hug and we fell to the sand laughing! "This is the best!"

David jumped back up and started dancing shouting about how good God was. I got it now. This is why he didn't need drugs anymore. I hadn't expected anything but had been willing to give it a try and God had met me with a sign from his own creation to seal the deal. Maybe my luck was turning for the better. This God and Jesus thing was real.

A few Weeks Later - Grants Pass, Oregon

Where was everybody? I made my way up some stairs in this little church my mom had suggested I go to for a prayer meeting. I'd come home to get some things. David and I were going to move in together again. I had heard voices from an upper room. I saw a door ajar and peeked in. It was a room full of praying people, that's for sure. A bunch of ladies in the middle of the day talking to God. A few nuns too from the Catholic church nearby. I snuck in quietly and took an empty seat.

I listened as they all took turns praying. It was a lot like talking. Talking to a great big Father in the sky that loved them. Is this how prayer worked? There weren't any rosaries or memorized rote words to pray?

"I just feel there is somebody here today we need to pray for." An elderly woman locked eyes with me.

"I'll take it!" I gladly agreed. I was hungry to understand more of this new faith I was walking in. They gathered around me and I closed my eyes. Suddenly something filled me. It was a massive presence and felt like every corner of my being was getting infiltrated by an unseen force. Joy bubbled up inside me and I laughed out loud. Was this what life with God felt like? I couldn't even focus on the ladies' prayers or what they were saying. This was better than any drug I'd ever taken in my life! The Holy Spirit had come upon me!

A Week Later - Faith Center - Eugene, Oregon

David was still sulking in the seat next to me. He hadn't wanted to come back to this place but the people I'd met in Grants Pass had told me to come visit this church when I got back to Eugene.

"That's just churchianity. What we are after is a relationship with the person of Jesus." The pastor shared, as he paced the small little stage in the middle of the gym. The person of Jesus. I was enthralled with this person of Jesus in my life. I couldn't wait to tell more people about him. My girlfriend had thought I'd gone crazy. I'd been not so sure how my parents felt about us getting all Protestant on them. Or was this Pentecostal? Were they Baptist? I didn't know what this place was, nor did I care. As soon as I'd walked in I'd felt that same wonderful presence and it'd filled me again. David could get over himself.

"We're coming back for the evening service, bro!" I whispered in his ear as the pastor continued his message.

1975 - The Hills Outside Lane Community College (Two Years Later)

Vroom! Pastor Roy's motorcycle sprayed me with mud as he zoomed by at an insane speed. I twisted the throttle and accelerated. I wasn't going to be the one to fall behind! Jim and Ray were taking up the lead. I laughed at the strangeness of the image. A pastor out here racing motorbikes with his staff. I sped up a hill and caught air on the way down. I'd never in my life imagined my spiritual leader would be doing an activity like this with me.

All the priests I'd grown up with I'd never even seen out of a white collar or the holy church setting with its stained glass windows contributing to a glorious atmosphere. Roy really was just an ordinary guy like the rest of us.

David and I had a bunch of men living with us now. We were always doing interesting things. Dumping ice water on unsuspecting sunbathing friends in the yard or pitching up a white sheet and projector to watch last week's baptisms etc. The Bible studies at the house were awesome. The instruction I was getting from church was phenomenal. As they say, I was growing like a weed, spiritually!

How had a guy like me with nothing left to live for found a love from a merciful God that would wipe my slate clean? How had He spared me in the car crash and the war? How had I gone from one of the most unlucky guys to a man of growing character and friends that had my back? How had my brother been so transformed I hardly recognized him anymore. We had joy now. We had freedom. We had a boldness from the Holy Spirit and I didn't want to live my life any other way.

I'd been volunteering with Sunday School and those kids were inspiring. They hadn't messed up their lives with drugs, sex, and alcohol, they had a fresh future ahead of them. They were the next generation and I loved sharing stories of Jesus with them. They needed to know what his love was like from an early age. If I could help with that I wanted to!

My friends had all stopped at the top of the next hill and were taking in the view. I pulled to a stop next to them. It was a merciful loving God that created all this. That had still seen me in my wallowing despair and saved me from suicide. I didn't live with the shame anymore. I didn't deserve it but it was there as a gift I couldn't earn and I'd said yes. Yes to Jesus. I was free.

**_Therefore, since we have been made
right in God's sight by faith, we have
peace with God because of what Jesus
Christ our Lord has done for us._**
Romans 5:1

Dennis went on to help mentor many of the young men that came into his and David's house. He started teaching Sunday School at Faith Center and found a love for teaching children. He went back to college and got a teaching degree. He was a teacher for twenty-seven years. Inspiring the next generations with his Mr. Rogers impersonation story times, and other character voices. He married Mary and they had four children. She died from breast cancer while their daughters were still in high school. Eight years later, he married Patti. They live in Springfield, Oregon and attend Eastside Baptist church. They have seven kids and eleven grandkids between them.

Dennis in the Air Force

Dennis

Dennis at the rock of his salvation experience.

Chapter 20

Highschool Dropout

Mike's Story

1973 Grants Pass Oregon

I'd thought dropping out of high school last year was the best idea ever. Now I wasn't so sure. I might need a plan B. I took another hit of the joint in my hand, closed my eyes and relaxed. This was life, right here. What did I need a high school diploma for anyway? Why did I need school at all?

"Here, man," I offered the joint to my friend sitting next to me.

He waved it off. "Nah, I got saved last night."

"From what?" I had no idea what he was talking about.

"Why don't you come to church with me tonight and see for yourself?"

"Sure man, why not?" This was going to be hysterical.

I grabbed my coat, anticipating the experience of religion while still high. I walked into my friend's church and saw a young guy in a leisure suit up on the stage talking. I tried not to laugh, but this was ridiculous.

As the music and singing started, I blinked my eyes, trying to clear my head.

But there was nothing to clear.

"Behold what manner of love..." the people around me were singing, and I suddenly felt out of place. My buzz had vanished!

I turned around to find the exit door calling my name.

This wasn't the plan.

I wasn't a church guy!

Instantly sober at the drop of a hymn wasn't my idea of fun.

How that was possible was beyond me.

But I was stuck in the middle of a row next to the friend who'd invited me, and I couldn't leave without drawing attention to myself.

The worship ended and the young man in the leisure suit started talking about Jesus.

The more he talked, and the more I sat here with a clear head, the more I realized that he was making sense. I was starting to believe him.

Jesus had to be the answer to the questions swirling through my mind.

He offered us an invitation to respond to the message and I said yes.

I wanted to try this Jesus thing.

1974 - 13th St - Eugene Oregon (One Year Later)

I slowed my bike to a stop at the intersection of Grant Street and waited for the light. I was taking classes at Lane Community College now, having moved down here with my friend, Tim Murff. We weren't living the Christian life any more, even though his mother thought we were. He'd come to church with me after that day I'd said yes to Jesus but we'd only lasted two weeks in the faith before slipping back into our old habits.

The light changed and I kept going east on 13th. Tim's mom would grab our hands and tell us to pray with her for things that would come up and we awkwardly fumbled through it as best we could muster with a fake faith. It kind of killed me inside, the duplicity I was exhibiting with her.

A parking lot filled to bursting with cars was quickly approaching on my right. I came to a screeching stop when I saw the little sign in the grass next to some steps that read FAITH CENTER.

Wasn't that the church Tim's mom told us we should go to here in Eugene? Was it really this popular? Church on a Sunday night? More cars were turning into the already packed lot. Was Sunday morning not good enough for these Christians? I was going to check it out. I tucked my bike in behind the steps and followed the crowd inside to a large carpeted gymnasium.

The music wasn't rock-'n-roll but it was only partially lame. I found a seat at the back and was shocked to see other people like me. The dude three rows in front had super long hair! The guy to my left had flip flops on and overalls! No matter what row of seats I looked down, the long-hairs were everywhere! And they weren't high or mocking the proceedings--they were sincerely engaging.

A short, brown-haired guy by the name of Roy Hicks, Jr. got up on a makeshift stage at the other end of the room and gave a simple message about Jesus. The same Jesus I'd walked away from. As if he was looking into my heart he said, "If you find yourself on the wrong path, but decide to give Jesus the final say in your decisions, He will lead you to the right path, even if you're heading the wrong way right now."

Was I on the wrong path? Was stopping here part of God guiding me back on the right one?

"If you want to recommit to Jesus being Lord of your life would you pray with me?" He bowed his head and closed his eyes and the room that was echoing his words around its domed ceiling became silent.

I whispered his prayer under my breath.

I wanted this.

I wanted to experience this new way of living.

I needed to give Jesus full access to my life.

Several months later

Dennis Ford hung up the phone. "That was the church asking if we could help a neighbor. Who wants to go pick up a sweet old lady from the nursing home down the street and take her to church on Sunday nights? She's in a wheelchair and it's gonna take two people to get her in and out of the car." Ray Meeks, David Ford, Tim Murff, and I stared at Dennis blankly. I had quickly moved out of my old living arrangements, trying to give this faith my best effort. Surprisingly, being in community with other guys who were following Jesus was changing me. The teachings at church and Jim Thomas' Saturday morning Bible studies with us were so practical and understandable that it wasn't so hard to start down new pathways, surrounded by other guys my age with similar goals. All of us were coming out of the same crazy '70s lifestyle.

Something Roy had said recently still resonated in my heart, "You're responsible for your obedience, Jesus is responsible for the outcomes."

"Mike?" Dennis was staring at me.

"I really don't do nursing homes. I hate the smell of old people and urine. It gives me the creeps," was the best excuse I could think of.

David listed off his responsibilities and so did the other guys. Why hadn't they asked me last? I could've come up with something better!

"Well Meeks brothers, it looks like it's going to be you two!" Dennis gave us a nod.

I rolled my eyes.

This was going to be great. Just great.

A few Sundays later

Ollie Peterson grimaced in pain as Ray helped ease her legs down into the space in front of the passenger seat. She let out a big, audible sigh of relief when the effects of arthritis from the wheelchair transfer had passed. Ray loaded her chair into the back of the car and Ollie smiled at me.

"Hey Mike, I got a new roommate!"

That meant someone was about to meet Jesus. This woman I had been so very resistant to helping a few weeks ago had humbled me with her stories every Sunday since. Here was an amazing Jesus follower, suffering in pain daily from severe arthritis and she got excited when she got a new roommate. Most every person who came into her room was on their way out. Ollie would tell them about the love of Jesus and they would go on to heaven soon after.

"They don't know what's coming for them Mrs. Peterson! I can't wait to hear about how it goes next week." I smiled at her as Ray hopped in and we started out of the parking lot.

"Boys, the Lord visited me last night."

I saw Ray's eyebrows rise in the rearview mirror.

"What do you mean?" I asked.

"I woke up, but I wasn't in my body. I was in the room looking down and then I rose through the roof and above the city and I could tell that the Lord was there with me."

"You what?" I asked, totally dumbfounded. What on earth was she describing? Had she died?

"I asked the Lord, are you taking me home? And He said, No. I'm just giving you a break from the pain. You're not done yet. Then I woke up in my body this morning and thought, I guess I'm getting a new roommate. And sure enough they wheeled a new dear soul into my room."

Ray and I were silent. A line of people out the window at the gas station waiting for fuel distracted me. Gas was at $1.00 now. The whole oil embargo overseas chaos was affecting us here in Eugene too. I didn't know what to say about Mrs. Peterson's experience as we pulled into the church parking lot.

As much as I'd hated the idea of being a chauffeur initially, this old woman was challenging my faith in so many good ways. If she could stick with Jesus through dying roommates and arthritis pain, what on earth did I have to complain about?

"Let's go worship." Ollie smiled.

1975 - Faith Center

"Mike Meeks, would you come up here?" Roy asked over the mic in front of the packed Sunday night service. My heart skipped a beat. But I found my limbs moving in obedience as the entire auditorium stared at me. I didn't know what was coming but if I had to guess it was probably something to do with a recent college retreat skit I'd done impersonating Roy.

I stood next to my pastor on the stage and he held up a handmade cardboard sign with my name on it. MIKE MEEKS. The string was a makeshift lanyard and he looped it over my neck.

"I know you've been playing different roles recently and I just want you to wear this through the service to remind you of your identity." Roy gave me a good natured "dirty look" as the gym erupted in laughter.

This was not the time for a clever comeback... I just needed to take it with a grin and move on. Roy waved me off the stage with a smile. I walked back to my seat as he began his sermon.

Funny, but I realized I finally did know who I was--and whose I was.

I was created and loved by God.

I belonged to Jesus and I belonged to this eclectic community of believers.

I was learning how to step out in faith and let Jesus be responsible for the outcomes.

And I was in this for the long haul.

> **"...being confident of this, that he who began a good work in**
> **you will carry it on to completion**
> **until the day of Christ Jesus."**
> **Philippians 1:6 NIV**

Mike never finished high school or college or even the Ministries Institute at Faith Center. Mike married his wife Carmen a few years later and went with their four month old son and Ken & Jan Klein to plant a church in Kirkland, WA. He served in various associate pastor roles over the next seventeen years while also growing a business. The church grew quickly and ended up merging with a church plant in Bellevue, Washington, led by Doug Murren and his wife, Debbie after the Kleins left to start their own outreach ministry. Mike and Carmen's daughter was born in Kirkland, WA and grew up surrounded by lots of love in this church family. Twenty years later, Mike has a defining shift in his calling, as recorded in the Epilogue, following the next chapter.

Mike

Mike and his wife Carmen.

Chapter 21

Roy's Story Part 3

1975 - Faith Center - Eugene, OR

The traffic from thirteenth street out my window in this furthest corner office distracted me. "Good morning Nita!" Cindy Meek's pleasant voice greeting our bookkeeper drifted down the hall to my office as I sat behind my desk looking through the day's to-do list. It was surprising to hear them exchange any words. Cindy must've taken our talk last week to heart. She'd come in here frustrated that Nita wouldn't speak to her and she didn't know why and I'd told her to just love her. She'd walked out not fully convinced it would do anything or knowing where to start but hearing her try now a week later was beautiful. I heard her footsteps approaching the doorway and looked up from my calendar.

I raised my eyebrows in silent curiosity.

"Roy told me I should just pretend to love her even if I didn't know how so I'm trying it." She answered my unspoken question and then looked down at the notepad in her hand.

"You need to leave by two PM today to make it to Portland for your speaking engagement tonight, and Dan Purkey called asking if he and Riley Taylor could tag along with you on your drive?" She changed the topic.

"Yes, I can swing by Lib House and pick them up on my way out. Is there anything else on the schedule today I'm missing?"

"Nope all good, but we in the office are wondering what to tell people that keep calling asking why all the young people are coming to our church?"

I constantly turned down requests from news outlets for interviews and comments. I didn't want to be the focus of attention or to put us up on some sort of pedestal. We were just following Jesus. "Jesus. Just tell them it's Jesus." I didn't even have to think about the answer to that one. There isn't any other explanation to what was happening here. We were being referred to as the granola church because when we hosted a meeting for the local pastors we always served granola. It might be an apt name as well of the types of people that would show up to the services and the Bible studies, even though in reality we had a great mix of granola and straight people. It amazed me what Jesus was doing in this place. I never would have imagined it. We'd had to build wings to the "sanctuasium" as it was so fondly referred to.

Cindy smiled as she wrote down my one word Sunday school style answer. There really wasn't a formula other than following Jesus. "Also, Roy, that guy called again, for the seventh time wanting to speak with you."

"How did he sound?"

"Well he wasn't very nice..."

"Then I don't want to talk to him." If someone couldn't be patient and courteous to my staff they could get help from someone else. Cindy looked almost relieved at my decision. It was important to me to have boundaries that protected my staff as best as I could. I remembered a few weeks ago when I'd gotten frustrated with something in the office and hadn't been the kindest to work with. Conviction had hit me and I'd sent Cindy a card to apologize for my monster ways. I didn't want to see myself respond like that again.

"Last thing is a church in South Africa called asking if you'd come and speak there." Her eyes were wide, noting the significance of the international call.

"South Africa!? You sure they wanted me? Not my dad?" It did happen. We shared the same name. I was just the short five foot six inch guy with a church in a remodeled gym. I really wasn't an Aimee Semple McPherson. Kay and I had been discussing how it was really time to start sending people out to plant their own churches. We weren't about building our own kingdoms. Many of our up and coming young leaders had been asking about going to Bible college but I knew what was going to be taught in those places. And if the Lord was leading them, great. But it also could be that we needed to support these guys better in the local church with training so they could go and plant their own pastorates. So they could go to the nations.

"I'll pray about it." She nodded and left as I scribbled some notes down on a scratch piece of paper. I frequently told people asking about getting into a public ministry to stay out if they could. I wasn't bitter towards it. It wasn't a statement out of cynicism, although it's possible people could interpret my words that way. I sure liked my sharp pithy statements but I also understood they might be overstated sometimes.

To church-plant, though, I understood the need to raise up leaders. There were so many leaders in our church already. This was in no way a one man show. Gratitude filled my heart as their faces flashed before my eyes, some old, many young, some new to Faith Center, some had been here since the beginning, others had already flown the nest. There was clearly a bigger need though with all of these interests in going to Bible colleges, but I didn't want them to end up in "churchianity" as I liked to call it.

What about a ministry school?

A Faith Center Bible school?

A Bible institute maybe.... a Ministry Institute....

1976 - "Sanctuasium" - Faith Center - Eugene Oregon (One Year Later)

"And the kingdom of God is not a spiritualized compartment in our lives. Sometimes we think when we're in church we're closer to the kingdom." I paced across the raised platform we'd constructed on the newly green carpeted gym floor, finishing my sermon about life in the King's domain. I stopped in the middle. "Afterward we go home to a difficult marriage or to a terrible job or to challenging kids. But the 'sphere of influence' of the King's domain covers EVERYTHING." Looking back down at my Bible on the podium I continued my thought. "Whatever we surrender to Jesus as King becomes His kingdom. Marriage, parenting, businesses, our own heart and mind."

I looked back up at the almost thousand people in the room, "Remember that Jesus taught us to pray, 'Thy kingdom come, Thy will be done.'" I pointed to the curved roof sarcastically to make the next point. "And He wasn't talking about a pie-in-the-sky, somewhere-down-the-line kingdom."

The gym filled with giggles. I smiled, then finished with the plea and heart of the message I hoped to drive home. I clasped my hands together. Pausing.

"Follow after Jesus......Embrace His Lordship daily. Live today as a child of the King." I spread my arms open in an invitation. "His kingdom is immediately available to you if Jesus is immediately King."

"I'd like to invite the elders to come up and if you want to respond to Jesus come down to the altar." The musical ministers started to play a slow melody as dozens of people came forward making their way down the riser steps on the left and right of me. This was normal now.

A typical Sunday evening service would see healings, multiple salvations. The testimonies humbled me. To get to be a part of this, as introverted as I was, it was humbling. We were so full we had built wings to the gym to hold everyone; the carpet had also been updated from orange to green finally.

My eye caught a young woman running down that new green carpet in the aisle waving her hands in the air and it didn't look like the typical response we'd get to an altar call. Disruptions weren't uncommon. We had a great usher team to work with them. Many of the people in the front here were already weeping as Jesus met them where they were. As I paced the stage waiting for the Lord to give me any further direction for worship or ministry, this same girl distracted me. I followed her gaze to a young man slowly pushing his way through to the front of the stage. I had heard a little about the girl, someone had mentioned to me she'd refused to sleep with her boyfriend and continue to sell drugs with him since coming to our church and giving her life to Jesus. I wonder if this was the boyfriend? I locked eyes with him.

The hair on the back of my neck stood up as he approached the few steps that separated us.

Something was off here. God what are you doing, what do you have for this young man?

Something glared in his eyes like a raging fire.

Was it hatred I saw? His left foot took the first step and he stopped.

"Jesus..." I whispered under my breath, turning off my mic so as not to draw attention to the situation.

Clunk!

My gaze was drawn to the source of the sound on the stairs. A knife lay there as if it had fallen from this young man's hand. I looked back up at his face that seemed frozen now versus full of rage, realization dawning on me.

This young man had been headed up here to kill me!

"Oh Jesus." I said audibly this time and maintained eye contact. His face was changing and he wasn't moving any closer as if an invisible force was stopping him. Tears started to form in his eyes as one of the elders came up the steps and started praying over him. He fell to his knees on the stairs just feet from where I stood and I felt the peace from the presence of the Lord wash the adrenaline away that had flooded my system.

Letting the man have his moment with the Lord, I took a step back to process. Maybe the staff suggestions of designated ushers as bouncers and a dedicated parking spot were more out of safety concerns than I thought. Maybe there was some wisdom there, Lord. Sure we had had threats and disturbances but this was new.

My times are in your hand God. I know where I go when I'm done here.

My heart filled with sorrow for those that didn't know where they were going after this life. How many people in this country now rejected even the existence of God! I recalled my youthful zeal of Bible college days when Jim and I had heard a proponent of atheism on the radio. By some miracle I'd called into the syndicated talk show and gotten on the air and been given the opportunity to defend the existence of my God for a whole thirty minutes. The radio host had ended our conversation with, "I'm glad you called. You've said some things that challenged me."

My mind returned to the present situation, "Jesus minister truth to this young man's soul. Bypass the lies that this culture has poured into him," I whispered a prayer as I meandered closer to where the would-be attacker was being ministered to.

"Jesus forgive me, come into my heart..." I heard a salvation prayer on his lips!

Praise the name of Jesus! Someone with a possible heart of murder and every opportunity to execute it had just been stopped by the sovereign hand of God and gotten saved instead!

Joy surged in my spirit as I took my exit for the night knowing the end of the service was in good hands with my staff. Sundays were long days. I was ready for bed. I collected my Bible off the podium and handed my mic to our sound tech on my way off the stage.

It was another good day with Jesus on the throne.

1986 - Eugene Faith Center (Ten Years Later)

The congregation sat in our not so new auditorium we'd built a few years ago listening attentively to Steve Overman preaching on what set a church up for long term fruitfulness. "Therefore, brethren, seek out from among you seven men of good reputation, full of the Holy Spirit and wisdom, whom we may appoint over this business..."[1] he read from the pulpit. The acoustics in the new auditorium were very flat compared to the echo the gym had provided us for so many years. But the stair step pews in the round and massive exposed beams the speakers hung from in here all made for a much easier and comfortable experience. There's something incredibly humbling watching leaders like Steve grow in this space.

I remembered him vaguely first arriving in the early 70s and getting confronted by one of the congregation about cleaning up his language. He'd been a brand new believer and grown in his faith rapidly. I also remembered him wanting to join me as we recorded video teachings for the Koinonia television show. It was a great medium for sharing the gospel although there had been that one time a large burly man at the gas station I'd tried to avoid eye contact with had come up to me asking if I was the guy on television. I'd nervously told him yes and he'd squashed me with the biggest hug and thanked me for my messages. I really didn't like the attention but if it was connecting with people outside the four walls of the church then it was worth doing. I tuned back to what Steve was saying. He'd gone on to Bible college and now here he was teaching a really relevant sermon.

---

1. Acts 6:3

"Apostles Peter and John weren't going away but new generations of ministry needed to be recognized and released like we then see Stephen do in chapter seven and Philip do in chapter eight."

Something about this message had a finality to it in my spirit. I had grown to know that nudge as one where I needed to listen to what the Holy Spirit was trying to say.

Words from one of my own teachings came back to me...

We come to moments in life where the torch is passed from one person to another, from one generation to the next. A man or woman of God senses in his or her heart that God is assigning a new task—and giving the necessary power of His life to accomplish that task. I am constrained by the Holy Spirit to offer you a possibility this may be your moment. Now may be the time when you should stir the gift He has deposited within you and prepare yourself for the moment when the torch will be passed...to you....

I've done this, haven't I God...

This is the next period of this church.

I watched as Steve walked across the stage with confidence and zeal.

I'm done.

A sudden sense of relief flooded me.

I had run this lead pastor race.

I had surrendered all those years ago in my own Bible college drop out days and chosen to take that which had been invested in me and did the best I could, even when it wasn't what I had initially envisioned. I had made mistakes. There are things I would've done differently now in hindsight. Taught differently. Spent more time with my son and Kay. But God had been so gracious and kind to me.

Multiple other churches had now been started in the Pacific Northwest. It was hard to see people go, people like Joe & Laina Wittwer, Kip & Pam Jacob, Rob & Joyce Tucker, Mark & Linda Wilson, Wayne & Anne Cordeiro, and so many others. I missed them and still heard from them frequently with questions as they pastored their own churches and yet we still grew. We were attracting up and coming musical talent like the girl Amy Grant in the white overalls that had blessed us with her sweet worship and voice a few years ago. Or the group Second Chapter of Acts.

My thoughts wandered back to my now nine year old son Jeff. How amazing it was to have been given a son all those years ago. To be a father now. Jeff was the delight of Kay and our lives. The Lord had perfect timing. I wish my ministry schedule wasn't so packed that I could be with them more. I needed to prioritize that better. All the mission trips and speaking engagements. The seasons of three morning services. I was thankful so many of the leaders had felt the call to go and plant their own churches.

The relief settled further in my spirit, bringing with it that all too familiar knowing of, "yes." That I'd learned to distinguish as the Lord's confirming personal word.

Yes. I am done.

It is time to pass my own torch in this area. Leaders like Steve are the future of this church.

"Bless God..." escaped my lips silently and a peace settled on me again.

A peace I knew only came from the person of Jesus.

For to me, to live is Christ,
and to die is gain.
Philippians 1:21 NASB

Dr. Roy Hicks Jr. pastored at Faith Center two more years and in August 1988 handed the reins off to Steve Overman and took a position as the Director of Foursquare Missions International in Los Angeles, moving his family to California. He, Kay and Jeff moved back to Eugene a few years later while Roy still served in leadership in the denomination. Roy made frequent trips to and from L.A. This schedule strained the family dynamic with Kay & Jeff at home in Oregon. He purchased a small airplane to help with this commute and on Feb 10th 1994 he radioed into the Medford Airport that he was experiencing engine trouble. His airplane crashed into a cliff nearby and Roy instantly went to meet his Jesus. At that time Faith Center had grown to 5,000 members and had sent out young leaders to plant over sixty new churches in the Northwest. In 1988 when he stepped down as head pastor of Faith Center after 20 years at its head, it is estimated there were 16,0000 people worshiping Jesus each week in the church plants alone. His memorial service drew thousands from all over the world and is described by many as a wake up call to the spiritual investment that had been planted in them by Roy. A collection of his sermons was put together posthumously in book form called A Small Book About God.[2] Ron & Helen Baker visited the crash site a week or so after the accident and found the closest street access to the area was named gateway to heaven.

Faith Center still exists today in the same location on 13th and Polk St. It is currently pastored by Russel Joyce who took over after Steve Overman retired.

You can read Dan Purkey, Riley Taylor, Brian & Christina O'Grady's stories in Becoming Jesus People Volume 1.[3]

You can find Kay's story in chapter 3. Joe Wittwer's story in chapter 7, Ron Baker's story in chapter 4. Mark & Linda Wilson's story was recently published in a book

---

2. Roy Hicks Jr, "A Small Book About God," (Colorado Springs: Multnomah Books,1997).

3. Carissa Gobble and Riley Taylor, "Becoming Jesus People:True Stories of How Love Broke Through In The Jesus People Movement," (GPC Publishing, 2023), 9-12 & 149-154, 35-44, 1-8, 53-62.

by their children titled American Leftovers[4] and features more stories about Faith Center and the church the Wilson's planted.

Disclaimer: The stories in Roy's chapters were collected from his widow Kay, his younger brother Jim, and a few of his friends and staff: Steve Overman, Cindy Meeks, Brenda Berg, Dan Purkey, Pam & Kip Jacob. His recorded sermons and video teachings and book were also helpful material. Others were also consulted to vet the tone of the chapters to how they recalled Roy's personality. Some creative license was taken to fill in gaps.

Roy teaching in Fireside room Ministries Institute class.

Roy preaching in the new sanctuary

Faith Center staff, c. 1981. In the front row, Cindy and Ray Meeks (Mike's brother) are fifth and sixth from the left, and Kay and Roy Hicks are to their right. Steve Overman is third in the second row, and Kip and Pam Jacob are sixth and seventh in the third row. Noel Campbell, from Molly and Cheri's stories, is fourth from the right in the back row. Paula, from the first volume in Brian's story, is fourth in the front row.

Epilogue

February 10, 1994 - Hicks Family Home - Eugene, Oregon

I closed the door to the empty garage and my heart sank. It was late and Roy wasn't home yet. He'd been hoping to get back tonight so he could take Jeff to watch Pat Lyon play her cello in the symphony. It wasn't like him to be this late. I grabbed the phone and dialed the Thomas's home.

"Hello?" Linda Thomas sounded sleepy on the other end but I needed a friend right now.

"Linda, it's Kay Hicks."

"Is everything ok?" I could tell she was concerned now. I didn't normally call this late at night.

"I don't know. Roy was supposed to be here hours ago. He was flying back today from L.A." The fear that gripped my heart eased a little finally vocalizing it out loud to a friend.

"I'll be right over Kay." She didn't skip a beat.

"Thanks." I hung up the phone and sat back down on the sofa.

Jeff was still asleep. I didn't want to wake him. Teenagers needed all the rest they could get and I didn't want to worry him needlessly. It's possible Roy'd gotten delayed but this wasn't like him. To be this many hours late and not send a word?

"Oh God, where is he?" I wept a quiet prayer.

The Next Morning - Meeks Family Residence - Seattle, Washington

Who would be calling at 6 AM? I picked up the ringing receiver. "Hello?"

"Mike Meeks?" A woman's voice asked.

"'Tis he."

"It's Margie Waldo."

A friend of ours from our Faith Center days. My wife Carmen and I had left in 1977 to plant a church in Washington with Ken and Jan Klein. I'd tried to balance a full time job growing a business and explore pastoring but had wrestled with the need to jump full in. We'd sold our Washington home and moved to California where Fuller Theological Seminary had looked at my lackluster transcript and let me into their masters program on academic probation. It had to be God's favor that I graduated with that masters degree a few years later, having never gotten my high school diploma or my bachelors degree. We were now back in Washington in the Seattle area as associate pastors back at Eastside Foursquare Church. Everything I'd learned was leading me to think I should probably choose full time ministry for the long haul but I wasn't fully sure yet.

"I have some bad news..." Margie's crackly voice brought me back to the conversation at hand. "Roy's plane went down in the southern Oregon mountains last night. He didn't survive." I almost dropped the receiver as my stomach fell to my feet. The wind was knocked out of me. The most influential person in my spiritual life was gone? How was this possible?Margie explained a few things I didn't hear and we hung up. What would I do without him? God, what are you doing?!

A Few Weeks Later - Lane County Fairgrounds - Eugene, Oregon

There wasn't a dry eye in this place. I held Carmen's hand in solidarity as the service came to a close. Five thousand people filled the fairgrounds today. The news said it was the largest memorial service in the history of the state of Oregon. People had come from overseas to be here and honor a man that had influenced so many. Impacted thousands. His own words filtered through my mind. "When I'm gone, don't be thinking about me. Because I won't be thinking about you." But how could we not? How could anyone dismiss the influence of a man like Roy? How could we not remember and celebrate and wonder at who God was, through him, to all of us?

Roy made an investment in you. That still small voice of the Holy Spirit stirred in my heart. *Roy made an investment in so many of you who are here right now.* The parable of the talents in the book of Matthew sprang to mind. Each one had been given an investment and downpayment and were judged by how they spent, invested, or saved them. How had I stewarded what had been invested in me through Roy and Faith Center? Here I was still clinging to an associate pastor role unwilling to commit to a life of full time ministry. Not that there was anything wrong with that, but I could feel the truth of what the Holy Spirit was trying to tell me right now in this moment. It was time to make use of that investment to its full potential. After all these years of only being halfway in the ministry I couldn't leave this service without giving God my all.

Ok God. I'm ready to step into a lead pastor role. I'm ready to take what has been given and imparted to me and give it away to whatever extent you want me to.

I looked over at Carmen and saw the tears welling in her eyes. This was a turning point and I was glad to have her at my side. Something settled in my Spirit and a peace washed over me as I knew my internal decision had been the surrender the Lord wanted from me. I still couldn't imagine not having Roy to talk to or call up with a question but I did know the same Jesus that had guided Roy was also guiding me. It wasn't about Roy. It was about the person of Jesus. Jesus would have his reward.

My times are in Your hand...
Psalms 31:15 NASB

Mike did go on to take on a lead pastor role. He jumped around in various churches for a few years before he was asked by Jared Roth, a long-term friend from Faith Center, to meet with a three year old church plant looking for a new Sr. Pastor in Chula Vista, California with a hundred people attending meetings at EastLake High School. This church had a vision to build a "lighthouse church" in the midst of a growing community and had 3.5 acres to work with. Mike and Carmen fit right into the culture. They served at EastLake Church for twenty-seven years, watching thousands come to the Lord and their children grow up in its community. In 2017 Mike stepped down from the lead pastor role and passed the leadership baton to James Grogan. EastLake Church now has eight satellite campuses. Mike and Carmen still continue to attend and serve at this church. During its tremendous growth period Mike would preach eight times per weekend. He says he learned that if there is no time to use the restroom, then you're doing too many services. If his story is ever turned into a movie Mike thinks Brad Pitt is the obvious choice to play him.

Seven years after Roy's sudden passing in 1994 Kay fell in love with Roger Bourland, a widower. Roger & Kay married and currently reside in Eugene, Oregon. They have nine grandchildren, and a great grandchild between them both. She continues to recall how much grace was on her and Roy in those exponential growth years of the church and recognizes how much God guided them in that time.

Roy and his son Jeff

Kay, Jeff & Roy Hicks

Gift for Purchasing This Book

We are so thankful that you chose to purchase a copy of this book and wanted to show our appreciation by making available to you an online treasure - audio recordings of over 550 of Roy's teachings. These can be freely downloaded or simply listened to over the web. To be emailed instructions to access this archive, simply enter your email at the link below or by scanning the QR code.

Roy Hicks Jr Archive

Please Leave Us a Review

Thank you for reading this book, it was a full family project and we would love to hear from you! Reviews help the book reach more people that could be encouraged by these testimonies.

Please leave us a review on Amazon, Goodreads, or BookBub, so we can make future versions of this book, or future volumes, better.

Salvation Prayer

- -

If you are hungry for an encounter with Jesus and God the Father like the ones depicted in these stories and want to invite Him into your heart, pray this prayer out loud to God. Begin reading the New Testament and talking to Jesus, and find a local church where you can be encouraged to pursue Him.

Jesus, I believe you are the son of God and that you came and died on the cross for my sins and then rose again to life so that I might also live. Come into my heart; cleanse me of all my past sins. I give my life to you. Come and fill me with your presence. I want to know You Jesus, so show yourself to me and help me find other believers with whom I can follow You. Thank you for all that You have done and will do for me.

Acknowledgements

Not many people read this section of the book but one reader of the first volume did and messaged me saying how much love she could see conveyed in it. My hope is that the people I'm about to list feel honored for their contributions to this second volume. This is by no means a one woman show it takes a team.

Andy Gobble, you amazing partner in this life, how did I get so blessed to have you as my husband? I'm so grateful you waited that whole year for me to be open to the possibility of a relationship with you. Best decision ever! You are a one of a kind dad and spouse. You held down the fort on multiple weekends as I was in the writing process and also have been invaluable with all my technical formatting and website linking questions. You are amazing and I could sing your praises all day long. This project wasn't possible without you.

Riley Taylor, it was a sad day when I learned you weren't supposed to write another volume of stories with me. It was hard to think of doing it without you but I'm so grateful for the time you were able to give me in coordinating connections with the amazing people in this book. This book wouldn't be here without all your efforts and encouragement to me in the process. The joy of working on the first book and in a new way the second book is a core memory for me that will last a lifetime. Thank you for trusting me with your friends' stories and for believing in me.

Thank you to, Russ & Mary McCall, Stefan Grabianowski, Erik & Linda Sampson, Brenda Berg, Cindy Van Ordstand, Cheri Wilson, Kay (Hicks) Bourland, Nancy Cunningham, Kip & Pam Jacob, Jim Hicks, Ron Baker, Joe Wittwer, Mike Meeks, David & Dennis Ford, Thomas Hamman, Molly Wells, Dan Purkey, Cindy Meeks, and Steve Overman for letting me interview and tell your stories in this book. Thank you also to those that joined us for the facility tour in November and lent your stories and recollections of the place in the 1970s.

Thank you Nicole Pritchard for another wonderful book cover and marketing material. Thank you Bonnie Temple for proof-reading the edited manuscript. And thank you Michael Williams for taking on the mammoth editing project this was.

To the grandmas Lynn Gobble and Wendy Hoffman that helped watch my kids so I could finish editing, go to book launches and write the book, my many many thanks! I really can't do all the things I do without my army of grandmothers, including Lindsay Taylor, to help me.

To my kids who will read this when they are older and can understand the mature themes in this book. Thank you for sharing your mommy with another book project and cheering me on in the process. You are a big reason for why I want to preserve these stories.

For everyone that lent their professional voice in endorsement of this project, thank you! The authority you carry makes a way for my little book to reach the hands of those that need to hear and read its message.

To everyone on my book launch team, you guys are the real heroes! This book doesn't go far without the effort and love you poured in to spread the word. Thank you.

Laura Purkey thank you for your tireless energy in organizing a Eugene Book launch! You are amazing!

I couldn't finish out this section without a heartfelt thanks to Gary & Louise Miller that hosted me for not one but two uninterrupted writing weekends at their home in Eugene. Who knew how much a writer could accomplish with two dedicated work days and no toddlers waking up for naps or homeschool duties calling my name for half the day. Thank you for blessing me with your home and generous hospitality.

Last, only because He sees this as I write it and those before this acknowledgement don't, but definitely not least is my thanks to Jesus for changing the lives of the people in this book so dramatically. Christmas this year has felt like it has new meaning to me as the reality of the gift You are to the world sinks further into my spirit. It's because of You we tell these stories.

Other Books by Carissa Gobble

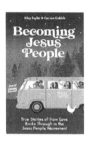  

Becoming Jesus People Volume 1

True Stories of How Love Broke Through in the Jesus People Movement

Turn The Bottle Over

How To Read Labels & Ask The Right Questions to Easily Detoxify Your Home

I'm From...Earth?

How Understanding Third Culture Kids Can Connect a Divided World

Made in the USA
Columbia, SC
16 February 2024

31711926R00148